WILLIAM BLAKE
AND THE AGE
OF REVOLUTION

CONTENTS

PLATES

INTRODUCTION:
THE TURBULENT AGE

ONE

History has a malicious trick of making little of what once seemed to be great events; and history will be no kinder to the heroics of our age than of others. Yet whatever in our century history slights, it will surely respect the domination of its two great wars— two wars which together have taken ten years out of our lives, and marked us with the hidden stigmata of violence and fear. In this, our age is like the age of Napoleon, which to-day, after the eagles and the magnificence, remains in the memory as Goya savagely pictured it: twenty-two years without conscience, stamping the men and the treasure of Europe into the dirt. So time will dwarf the mechanical glories of our century, but it will not lift their tragic weight from men's minds.

The name of Napoleon walks briskly into these reflections, and we see the likeness between his wars and ours at once. Nothing that compares with the Napoleonic wars or with ours happened in the hundred years between 1815 and 1914. They were not peaceful years for the empires of Europe: they spanned the Indian mutiny and the Crimean campaign, wars between France and Prussia, Russia and Japan, the South African and the Balkan wars. Yet these wars had always the air of another time: of encountering and not of shaping the daily lives of men. They do not compare with the convulsions that for a generation preceded Waterloo, and those which for a longer generation have followed the battles of Tannenberg and the Marne. They did not terrify their on-lookers as those who looked on at the Holy Alliance and at Munich stepped back in terror. They did not close upon the mind and the heart with iron hoops.

By contrast, from about 1760 to 1815 the minds of men were obsessed with revolution, and this gave to the struggles of that age (as of ours) the character of religious wars. We catch the tone at once in the literature of the time, and it makes the Romantic Revival direct and close to us; we are drawn to it because we share in our lives those hopes and heart-searchings, those shifts of loyalties, the same vacillations between principle and expedience. There is nothing like this in the earlier eighteenth century, whose Indian summer remains fixed in the solemn doggerel of Joseph Addison. And there is nothing like it later in the nineteenth century, whose Victorian calm is fixed in the gracious bombast of Alfred, Lord Tennyson. The poets who quicken our pulse and sound in our ears are those who struggled in the urgent years about 1800, because they were possessed by the same compulsions as possess us.

TWO

The turbulent age from about 1760 to 1815 was shaped, of course, by the American and the French Revolutions; and it was also shaped by the Industrial Revolution. There is a unity between all three of these: the movement of industry from the village to the factory was pushed on by the same forces that made the political movements. A common restlessness runs under that time, a discontent with the traditional ways of doing and thinking, and an urge to band men together in new alliances. The age of the revolutions was powered by common aspirations in its poetry and its politics, its ideals and its inventions, and as far apart as the organization of Napoleon's armies and of Richard Arkwright's factories.

The massive expansion of manufacture by machines about the year 1800 obviously changed the economy of England. And, more subtly, it changed the way in which men looked at the economy and at their own place in it. So long as men worked in villages, they thought of their livelihood as a gift: a gift from God or from nature, which God or nature might bless with plenty in one year and blast with famine in another. The cottage weaver at his loom thought in this way, even though the loom made the greater part of his living for him; he thought in this way because (as Daniel Defoe insists) he still turned to his patch of garden and his rights on the common land for a critical part of his living. A slump seemed as much an Act of God to him as a drought. The village worker did not think of himself as the master of his destiny, because his craft did not make up his whole possession.

The move to the factory and the enclosure of common land changed all this. They put the worker into a different place in his economy, to which he now had only one thing to give: the labour of his hands. No longer did a superhuman dispensation stand between his work and its reward. If the society of masters rejected his handiwork, and found no use for his skill and diligence, there was something wrong with society, and not with God or with nature.

It is strange to see that the spread of machines made the men who worked them conscious, first of their own work, and then of themselves as men. Yet this is what the Industrial Revolution did. It forced men in the long run to seek their destiny, and to find their station, not in the hand of God but in their own hands. In 1720, the village workers had accepted the slump that followed the South Sea Bubble as an accident of nature. In the slumps a hundred years later, the cloth-shearers and the stocking-knitters drilled on the dark moors in open mutiny against the economy that starved them.

The machines changed the organization of society, and shifted the centre of a man's life from his cottage home to the daily factory. In that shift, the man ceased to be a member of his family and his village, and in the long run became simply himself: a person. Because the machine in the factory changed the order in his life, it slowly changed the status of the worker who served it. It regimented and brutalized and starved him, it exploited him and (for a long time) his family, and it robbed him of everything but his skill. And yet, by these acts in the end it made him a man— a man alone.

This is the change of conscience which links the political revolutions to the rise of industry, and the American smallholder in 1775 to the Luddite of 1811. Here the citizens who proclaimed the Rights of Man in America and in France were at one with the tanners and the nailmakers who quoted from *The Wealth of Nations* by Adam Smith. They spoke with different voices, but they spoke for the same cast of mind, in the homely pamphlets of Benjamin Franklin, in the educational schemes of Rousseau and Jefferson, and in the romantic poetry of Robert Burns and William Blake and Wordsworth. We catch in all of them a new sense that the dignity of man is the simple dignity of labour, and a new image of man the maker.

THREE

Western society as we know it was made in the convulsions of the great revolutions, roughly between 1760 and 1815. In an obvious sense, the Industrial Revolution in those years forged the mechanical skeleton for our society. But it was not only the mechanics that were laid down then: the ancient orders of homage were sapped, as much in the English factory as in America and France; and as much by the self-made owner as by the factory hand. The social order had been fixed most sharply in England in the subservience of the villager to the landed gentleman. We can hear it break as sharply in 1775, when owners and workers alike openly sided with the American revolutionaries. The English opposition to King George's war shared a common sense that in America the sturdy sons of nature were in revolt against the lords of the manor. This was not a political union; its unity grew from a new imaginative concept of the dignity of man. It was a popular movement, in the literal sense: it paid tribute to people and not to lords —not to birth, not to rank, and not to inheritance. Like the upstart men who three hundred years earlier made the Renaissance in Italy, the leaders of the revolutions cared nothing about their lineage.

We are all conscious now that our society was first remade in the Renaissance; and yet we still miss the equal intellectual force in the Industrial Revolution. We have learnt from Jacob Burckhardt that the Italian Renaissance was not merely an invention in the arts. It was a watershed in history: it changed the flow of thought and action all through our civilization, in religion and daily life and politics, and most deeply in man's conception of himself. Indeed, since Burckhardt wrote we have learnt that the Renaissance ran even wider than he saw, for it also set going changes in technical skill and understanding which in time made a scientific revolution.

All this we have come to see in the Renaissance because it began more than five hundred years ago. But because the Industrial Revolution began only two hundred years ago, we still miss both its sweep and its depth; we still think of it as a set of ingenious inventions and no more. We owe this misreading, of course, to the bias in our education, which has made the history books shy away from industry as a vulgar practice whose spread into civilized life they ought to ignore—as they long ignored the science in the Renaissance. It will take us time to see that the Industrial Revolution changed the flow of thought and action throughout the West as largely and as deeply as did the Renaissance. It changed the bent of men's minds as well as the conditions of life, in politics and in housing, in poetry and in dress, in the flamboyant monuments of the evangelical sculptors and in the inventions of the Quaker ironmasters. Most deeply, the Industrial Revolution in the long run changed man's conception of himself. Like the Renaissance, it broke the forms of a classical culture, and set about making a popular taste of its own from new beginnings.

In the Renaissance, artists and cardinals and *condottieri* had once boasted that they were not born in a great bed. So the powerful minds of the Industrial Revolution, philosophers and inventors and captains of industry, were proud to say that they were born in a cottage. They were asserting a universal humanity, which made each man a person and a master: the master of his own fate. The Industrial Revolution, like the political revolutions which marched with it, put an end to men's resignation to the tyranny either of men or of nature. America and France threw off their kings, and in England the machines shook off the obstinate hold of an economy in which men had long wrestled for a bare livelihood.

FOUR

The revolutions in America and France were popular risings, in the nature of things. And it was also natural that when the risings turned into war, those who stayed to fight the long campaigns were ordinary people. This is the nature of revolutionary and religious wars, and yet it was new in the wars of the eighteenth century; for the troops whom the revolutionaries fought were not ordinary people.

The troops of that age were hired soldiers who were as remote from the affairs of their lords as the Swiss Guard is from those of the Pope. Now for the first time these professionals, who had fought parade skirmishes on behalf of their impersonal masters, stood in the field against a mob of farmers and labourers, and were defeated. When George Washington husbanded his men through the winter at Valley Forge, when Napoleon pushed his people's army through the Alps, they did more than rout the cautious mercenaries marshalled against them. They finally destroyed the standing—and the profession—of the personal guard.

The professional soldier had long been disliked in England; and yet there had clung to him an incense of admiration, a gladiator's aura of heroism. The glory of war had always been a classical theme, and it is unexpected that it should fade from English poetry in an age of bitter war. The reason is in the bitterness: when the citizen raised his rifle, and the drilled footmen broke ranks and followed their mounted masters into exile, the heroics went out of war. At the end of the wars of revolution, there were no laurels for the heroes, and no poems. The epic poem died before 1800. By a nice irony, its place as a narrative was taken by the novel, and the word 'hero' came to mean not a soldier but a lover.

We can date the death of the epic praise of war in England precisely. The last narrative poem of this kind was the translation by Alexander Pope of Homer's *Iliad*. Pope undertook this with much fanfare in 1713, when he was a bright young man of twenty-five, who had astonished the bigwigs of London for four years. Now he offered at six guineas the set to make his subscribers patrons, not of Pope, but of culture. Homer in the Augustan manner was to be the monument of eighteenth-century England, as deliberately as the *Encyclopédie*, forty years later, was planned to be the monument of eighteenth-century France.

What the eighteenth century called the Town took up the plan solemnly. The lords and the bishops, Bolingbroke and Atterbury; the bigwigs and the philosophers, Congreve and Berkeley; friends and enemies, Swift and Addison; dons and doctors, Young and Arbuthnot; the arts and the sciences, Wren and Newton; the wits, the belles, the politicians—all were subscribers. They were doing a serious social duty, for which Pope was the instrument; and they paid him handsomely, about £5,000 for the work. A whole society spoke for its culture in Pope's *Iliad*. In fact, however, the number of subscribers was 574.

Of course this number was taken from a smaller population than to-day's. To-day there are about eight million people in London; in 1713, there were not six millions in England. And few of these could read, and fewer spare six gold guineas. Nevertheless, 574 men was a handful: smaller, in its setting, than the Council of Athens. And this handful of men was Augustan society: the society which was surer than Athens that it was sane, lasting, the arbiter of knowledge and taste.

In that society, literary men were still close to the reins of power. The poet Matthew Prior had just negotiated peace with the French in 1711; and Pope's most constant friend, Jonathan Swift, was the granter of state patronage for a few years. All this was turned upside down later in the century, when war was endemic and yet the epic withered. The power and the patronage died together; and instead, the poets found their following among less gentlemanly readers. They read the religious verses of William Cowper, the cottage lyrics of Robert Burns, and the homely narrative of George Crabbe. In 1800, Robert Bloomfield (who is now remembered only because he influenced John Clare) wrote a poem *The Farmer's Boy* which sold 26,000 copies in three years. About the same time, two admirers of the French Revolution, William Wordsworth and Samuel Taylor Coleridge, put forward in the preface to the *Lyrical Ballads* the radical doctrine that the business of the poet was 'to choose incidents and situations from common life, and to relate or describe them, throughout, as far as was possible in a selection of language really used by men.'

FIVE

William Blake is to me the poet whose work and whose life express most sensitively the moving changes of that age. He more than any other had the ambitions of simple men, spoke out of their difficult dilemmas, and suffered their neglect. His poetry and his designs belong to the Romantic Revival, and his life and his friends (as well as the men he hated) belong to the Industrial Revolution. He was a man of the new stamp, self-taught, lonely, awkward, with none of the graces of the poets of the Augustan establishment; and he broke their formal tradition to pieces.

This book then is a study of one man, odd, unbending, wayward, and self-absorbed, whose mind was all visual and visionary. At the same time, because the man lived and thought so honestly, this is a book about an age: the turbulent age of William Blake. For though he was only an engraver by trade, and a poet by ambition, he belonged to the race of the driving, rising men, John Wilkes and Joseph Priestley, John Wesley and Benjamin Franklin, who made the world over into the modern form we live in. Everything that happened then, happened to William Blake. He expressed the hopes of the French Revolution in the lucid songs that he began in 1789. He went on writing as lucidly but bitterly against the English hatred of the Revolution at least until 1794. Only after Napoleon betrayed the Revolution, sometime towards 1800, did he finally settle into that endless monologue of fantasy about a Biblical hereafter which we call his prophetic books.

In these senses, this book is a study of one man in one age. But because the man was a poet and an artist, it is in the end a study of all poetry and all art. In the work of William Blake the wars and the famines, the shifts of policies and ideals, become the agonies of all ages; and the hopes of one man become the aspirations of all mankind.

What hopes he had, what quicksilver books he wrote, their headstrong amalgam of prophecy and heresy, the chapters that follow will tell. Yet there is something that should be said at the outset about the man himself. Blake has been pictured by his biographers as a forbidding and humourless patriarch, another bearded giant among the bigots and monomaniacs of his age. And

Blake was indeed a man of strong loves and hates and passionate principles. But he was not thereby less human. On the contrary, he was full of lively interests, was playful and quick-witted and witty, and had a happy confidence in himself that no authority could cow. Blake always gives the sense of a mind in flower. For example, he hated what seemed to him the materialist philosophy that runs from John Locke's *Essay Concerning Human Understanding* to David Hume. Yet when in his twenties Blake satirized their outlook (and his earnest friends who shared it), he could find a single pungent witticism for it: he called it,

An Easy of Huming Understanding, by John Lookye Gent.   52

This has the punning tricks of language and the teasing sense of criticism by ridicule which have only been revived by James Joyce in our lifetime.

Blake carried this bright gift into his serious work; he could always transform a solemn political commonplace into a personal quip. When James Gillray drew a cartoon (during the trial of Louis XVI in January 1793) which scoffed at Charles Fox as a foolish lover of liberty, climbing towards a waning moon with a ladder that is too short, Blake took fire at the sneer, but he did not rage at the turncoat. Instead, he simply lengthened the ladder, changed the moon over to its waxing phase, and turned Gillray's mock into the aspiration of one of his most poignant engravings, the plate 'I want! I want!' in *The Gates of Paradise*. Indeed, Blake calmly took that collective title for his plates from the cynical inscription in Gillray's cartoon, 'The Straight Gate or the way to the Patriot's Paradise.'

SIX

William Blake shared with other leaders of his age a distaste for the established ritual of the Church of England. He was a dissenter, like many of the Quakers and Unitarians whom he knew. But his form of dissent was more mystical than theirs, and derived (beyond Swedenborg) from a tradition which has been only recently and partly uncovered. It now seems likely that the roots of the religious and political dissent which Blake echoes run back into the Puritan Revolution of the 1640s, when for the first time a king was beheaded in Europe, and a new army and a new society were set up by Oliver Cromwell.

Several factions of Puritans had struggled for power in that earlier revolution, between 1640 and 1650. The more extreme of them were suppressed by Oliver Cromwell in 1649 and had to go underground. One such dissident faction, the Levellers led by Colonel John Lilburne, had been powerful in the army; and it also had a pacifist wing, the Diggers led by Gerrard Winstanley, who wanted to overthrow all ownership and to create God's kingdom, the New Jerusalem, on the pattern of the Apostles. These political ideas in religious dress were preached by several eccentric sects—the Anabaptists, the Fifth Monarchy men, the Seekers, the Ranters, and the newly formed Quakers—and remained alive throughout the eighteenth and into the nineteenth century. Their influence is evident, for example, in the later sects of Shakers and Owenites in America.

The men who carried on this hidden tradition used the language and the metaphors of the Old Testament as Blake uses them in his poems. For example, the secret doctrine of these mystical anarchists was called by them the Everlasting Gospel; and this is the title that Blake took for the moving and heretical verses in which in his last years he still wrote out his contempt (and theirs) for the authoritarian God of the Old Testament, and his love for Christ the rebellious child.

> He scorn'd Earth's Parents, scorn'd Earth's God,
> And mock'd the one & the other's Rod;
> His Seventy Disciples sent
> Against Religion & Government:
> They by the Sword of Justice fell
> And him their Cruel Murderer tell.
> He left his Father's trade to roam
> A wand'ring Vagrant without Home;
> And thus he others' labour stole
> That he might live above Controll.
> The Publicans & Harlots he
> Selected for his Company
> And from the Adulteress turn'd away
> God's righteous Law, that lost its Prey.

757

With these Gnostic heresies Blake as a young man held another strain of dissent, which now seems alien, and which indeed he gave up in his old age. This was the rationalist dissent of the Unitarian heretics, of whom Isaac Newton had been one long ago and Joseph Priestley was one now. The young Blake linked it with the underground tradition of the Diggers and the Ranters, for two reasons: a reason of the mind, and a reason of the heart.

The reason of the mind is easy to read. Rationalist dissent was also radical and anti-authoritarian, in politics and in religion. The Unitarian God was one with man, and so was Blake's God.

> God Appears & God is Light
> To those poor Souls who dwell in Night,
> But does a Human Form Display
> To those who Dwell in Realms of day,   434

he wrote in *Auguries of Innocence*.

The reason of the heart lay farther off. Blake loved the adventure of learning; to him, Christ was the wonder child and the symbol of knowledge, innocence at one with experience. He taught his young wife to read and write; and he was drawn to the rationalist dissenters because they cared for education. They were not admitted to the English Universities, and had therefore had to set up their own academies. Men and women from these academies were the friends with whom Blake worked in his twenties, and on whose moral verses for children he modelled his own *Songs of Innocence*. For example, Blake knew in London the famous blue-stocking Mrs Letitia Barbauld, who wrote books of instruction on every topic in literature and in science. Her father had been head of the great Warrington Academy, and had brought Joseph Priestley there to teach English and modern languages, which were new subjects not taught at the Universities. At Warrington, Priestley was drawn to even newer subjects, and became so interested in electricity and in chemistry that he is now remembered chiefly for his deep discoveries in these sciences—for example, for his discovery of oxygen. Mrs Barbauld probably, and Joseph Priestley certainly, are teased by Blake in his early satire, *An Island in the Moon*. It is Priestley, 'Inflammable Gass', who challenges the other philosophers with the cry 'Your reason—Your reason?' which Blake turned later

into the name for the God of materialism, Urizen, whom he
abhorred.

SEVEN

I have come to William Blake as the subject of my study because
his work unites the timeless with the timely, the sense of destiny
with the sense of the present. Like every great poet, he had the ear
which caught the whisper of the Everlasting Gospel in the everyday passions round him. It is the belief of great poets that the
condition of man expresses eternally the same themes of love,
of truth, of justice and dignity. Yet to the generation which lived
through the age of Napoleon and William Pitt, of Peterloo and
the Six Acts, the human condition was not an abstract play of
ideals; it was experienced in famine and oppression, in poverty and
neglect. This is why his age speaks so insistently to ours; for we
also, the generation of Belsen and Sharpeville and Stalin's corrupt
tyranny, have learnt that man's ideals of his own humanity have
still to be fought for in every age.

Of the seventy years of Blake's life, from 1757 to 1827, England
was at war for thirty-five. From the Seven Years' War through
the American Revolution to the French wars, they became less
and less the traditional skirmishes of men. They became more and
more international, ideological, and ruthless. They became the
economic wars of Napoleon's Decrees and the British Orders in
Council; they became total war. This is the sequence, step by step
more inhuman and more mechanical, which made Blake identify
his two hatreds—hatred of the dehumanized machine, and hatred
of war.

> And Los's Furnaces howl loud, living, self-moving, lamenting
> With fury & despair, & they stretch from South to North
> Thro' all the Four Points, Lo! the Labourers at the Furnaces,
> Rintrah & Palamabron, Theotormon & Bromion, loud lab'ring
> With the innumerable multitudes of Golgonooza round the
>   Anvils
> Of Death! But how they came forth from the Furnaces, & how
>   long
> Vast & severe the anguish e'er they knew their Father, were

> Long to tell; & of the iron rollers, golden axle-trees & yokes
> Of brass, iron chains & braces, & the gold, silver & brass,
> Mingled or separate, for swords, arrows, cannons, mortars,
> The terrible ball, the wedge, the loud sounding hammer of
> destruction,
> The sounding flail to thresh, the winnow to winnow king-
> doms,
> The water wheel & mill of many innumerable wheels re-
> sistless,
> Over the Four fold Monarchy from Earth to the Mundane
> Shell. 713

Behind the outlandish names, the link between Blake's imagination and his violent times is evident. If it has been missed in the
past, it can hardly be missed to-day. To-day the heavy sound in his
books of the loom and the forge has so plain an echo in our ear that
we hardly need to be told how good was Blake's ear. It was too
good. It followed the details of rebellion and repression, of industry
and war so faithfully that he could not but become first unpopular,
and then shunned and neglected.

Blake's indifference to his neglect by his contemporaries has been
mistaken, by more worldly readers, for indifference to the world. In
fact, it now becomes clear that he wrote his symbolic poems like a
diary, as much about the outer world as about his inner thoughts.
He put down in his prophetic books what he thought of Malthus's
theories of over-population in the same breath, and the same idiom,
as his thoughts about God. Since he was an exceptionally sensitive,
above all an imaginative observer, his background much of the time
is simply too wide for us. Moreover, we find it hard to understand
how the man who was a revolutionary until 1800 could have retreated into religious resignation after 1804. How could he, who had
once cursed the authority of Church and State, now protest only at
the Old Testament figure of Urizen?

We are no longer used to linking radicalism with religious fervour: in this, Blake was at the end of a Puritan tradition which we
have lost. Yet unless we can see as one the revolutionary idealism
in Blake's politics and the Gnostic heresy in his religion, we simply
do not see Blake. In his last prophetic book, *Jerusalem*, he still
wrote,

Are not Religion & Politics the Same Thing? Brotherhood is Religion.

689

And we do not see as Blake saw; we do not look with his visual mind, we do not hear with his direct and sensuous ear. Through all his poems, there sound the iron footsteps of the modern age: war, oppression, the machine, poverty and the loss of personality. They crowd the pages of his symbolic books as casually as a letter which sneers at Pitt or a marginal note which sides with Tom Paine. This is the prophetic power of Blake: that he felt the coming disasters of war, empire, and industry in his bloodstream, long before politicians and economists shivered at their shadows.

EIGHT

It is over twenty years since the body of this book was written in 1942. At that time, I was working every day of the week at the tasks of destruction which war sets for a scientist. I wrote about Blake when I could, usually late at night; and what I wrote had for me then the force of a commentary on my own day—a testament of what I valued at a time when I feared that it would be destroyed.

Indeed, at that time I did not expect to finish the book. Yet I was sure that I must start it; I had to record my sense of the dignity of an age, the great age of the Industrial Revolution, which had been overlooked or slighted by the historians of our culture. I wanted to speak up for a poet and his rationalist friends together, whose longings of intellect and emotion had made the modern world that I loved.

Of course, I am not the first man to have a new view of Blake. The liveliest book about him is also the earliest: Alexander Gilchrist's *Life of William Blake*, first printed in 1863. It has been ably edited by Ruthven Todd for the Everyman Library, with notes which add what has been learnt of Blake since Gilchrist wrote. Much of this new matter, and the old, has been presented by Mona Wilson in her centenary *Life of William Blake*. I am indebted to both these books, as well as to many other lives and commentaries. The sprightliest of the latter is again the earliest: Algernon Charles Swinburne's *William Blake, A Critical Essay*, which was printed in

1868. Of books which treat Blake as a mystic, the most searching seem to me to be Denis Saurat's *Blake and Modern Thought* and Milton O. Percival's *William Blake's Circle of Destiny*.

Blake's shorter poems were first edited with scrupulous detail by John Sampson in *The Poetical Works of William Blake* in 1905. Since then, Blake's complete writings—poems, prophetic books, and prose—have been magnificently edited by Geoffrey Keynes for the Nonesuch Press: first in three volumes in 1925; then in one volume without the variant readings in 1927; and most recently in a single volume with the variant readings. This last, *The Complete Writings of William Blake, With all the Variant Readings, published in 1957* is a good and convenient popular edition, and I have used it to revise the text of all my quotations from Blake. The number which follows each quotation is that of the page on which the bulk of the quotation stands in this edition.

When I wrote my book in 1942, Blake was regarded as an untaught and remote mystic whose poems lay quite outside his times and our tradition. I showed, in his life and in his writings, that his inspiration was both more robust and more universal than this, and that his vision never missed the meaning of the tremendous years through which he lived. Since my book was first printed, this more ample view of Blake has begun to enter the textbooks, sometimes with and sometimes without acknowledgement. More important, the researches of others have brought new evidence of Blake's informed, exact, and apt interest in his whole world. Among scholars who have demonstrated this are Mark Schorer in *The Politics of Vision*, Geoffrey Keynes in his *Blake Studies*, and Kathleen Raine in her continuing search into the sources of Blake's mystic knowledge. Two books in particular have filled in the outline of my book, and I have drawn on both of them in this Introduction: one is David V. Erdman's *Blake: Prophet Against Empire*, and the other is A. L. Morton's pioneer study of the secret Puritan tradition, *The Everlasting Gospel*.

THE PROPHETIC MASK

ONE

William Blake was born on 28 November 1757; he married Catherine Sophia Boucher on 18 August 1782; and he died about six in the afternoon of 12 August 1827. We know little more of his life. A poet whose poems were unknown; a painter whose painting was disliked: he would have been glad to salvage something less than a life, a living. For Blake had not chosen to be a poet and a painter. At fourteen Blake had chosen to be an engraver; and he held to that choice until he died. He served seven years as an apprentice; he engraved for booksellers; he ran a print-shop. His friends were the men with whom he worked: the designer Thomas Stothard, the sculptor John Flaxman, the painter Henry Fuseli. They helped him to find work and patrons, and they did what little was done to make his poems and his painting known. Blake was nearly forty before he was asked to engrave the first large book of his own designs, to Edward Young's *Night Thoughts*. It was printed in the slump of 1797, and failed. Thereafter Blake seldom had enough even of hackwork, and lived when he could by patronage. A second book of his designs, to Robert Blair's *The Grave*, was printed in 1808; but it had been given to another to engrave. Blake held a show of his paintings through the summer of 1809. It failed. We do not know how he lived for the next ten years. The slumps had deepened; inflation and unemployment were growing unchecked; Blake was an old man who felt himself shouldered out of work. One by one he quarrelled with the fellow craftsmen who had been his friends. He was lucky after 1818 to find friends in their place, among younger painters who happened to be religious cranks. Their leader, John Linnell, got the Royal Academy to give Blake £25 in 1822. But to keep Blake alive, he had to commission most of his work. Only thus did Blake at last salvage half a dozen years of passable comfort and dignity. He used them to make his best engravings, for *The Book of Job*, and his finest designs, for Dante's *Divine Comedy*. Yet when *Job* was printed, a year before Blake died, it failed.

It is a story to put its age to shame: decent, humdrum, and hopeless. But it is not an uncommon, it is not even a personal story. Blake lived the impersonal life of a craftsman, using his hands as he had been taught, and keeping his mind his own. The disaster was not in his gifts but in the everyday of his world; the disaster was the world. Change marched masterfully and marched violently through his world: this crippled his livelihood, and this cowed him and made him helpless. There is nothing odd in what happened to Blake; for it was happening to many thousand others. The fine London watchmakers were becoming hands in sweat-shops. The learned societies of the Spitalfields silk-weavers were rioting for bread. The small owners were losing their place, and their skilled workers were losing their livelihood. It is a murderous story, and it is Blake's story. But it is not the poet's story, nor the painter's. It is the story of Blake the engraver.

Blake had become an engraver, at a fee of fifty guineas, as he might become an advertising draughtsman to-day: because he could not afford to become a painter. He may have hoped to work his way from craftsmanship to design. So, in the generation before his, Clarkson, the elder Catton, and John Baker had first worked as coach painters. So, in Blake's own generation, Stothard had drawn patterns in Spitalfields; and Flaxman designed pottery for the Wedgwoods. But when Blake was apprenticed, the English painters had just won the social standing which they had long coveted; and had at once shut out the engravers. Hogarth had set his face against an English academy all his life, because he feared this rift. But Hogarth had died in 1764. In 1768 his Society of Artists, to spite its bigwigs, chose another one-time coach painter for president. The bigwigs walked out and founded the Royal Academy, with Joshua Reynolds for president. Engravers could not become members of the Royal Academy. When later the Academy allowed them six lesser seats as associates, the engravers fought back by not putting up for them. This is why Blake's bitterness, at fifty, against Reynolds's *Discourses* to the Royal Academy, is aimed above all at their smugness.

> The Enquiry in England is not whether a Man has Talents & Genius, But whether he is Passive & Polite & a Virtuous Ass & obedient to Noblemen's Opinions in Art & Science. If he is, he is a Good Man. If Not, he must be Starved. 453
> Liberality! we want not Liberality. We want a Fair Price & Proportionate Value & a General Demand for Art. 446
> This Whole Book was Written to Serve Political Purposes. 451

And Blake's dislike of the classical manner of the Royal Academy was of a piece with this social anger. Blake had been apprenticed to James Basire, one of a family of craftsmen, engravers to the Society of Antiquaries. Here he learned the growing fashion, to set store by old things: among them Basire's rather old-fashioned style. To-day we recall this as the fashion of a nobility gracefully mourning its decay. But the dislike of the vulgar Court which this Gothic taste spoke was not the monopoly of exquisites like Horace Walpole, privately printing Gray's *The Bard*. A print of 1771, which shows Welsh counties paying homage to John Wilkes, has the verse,

> Thus Ancient Britons, gen'rous, bold & free,
> Untaught at Court to bend the supple Knee,
> Corruption's Shrine with honest Pride disdain
> And only bow to Freedom's Patriot Train.

For the newly made folk-lore of a Druid Albion had also been seized by those who fought George III's Court more robustly. The Freemasons, the Ancient Family of Leeches, the small men who made Wilkes and Liberty a symbol for their discontent, took the Ancient Britons for forefathers of their brotherhoods. It was their Gothic, not Walpole's, which Blake made his own; it had for his age the same force that primitive art has had for ours. When later, in the French wars, not long after the end of the *Albion* newspaper, Blake painted *The Ancient Britons*, he saw them

naked, simple, plain in their acts and manners; wiser than
after-ages. They were overwhelmed by brutal arms.   577

TWO

I make it plain at the outset that, in the social struggle of that time,
my sympathy is with Blake. But I must make it as plain that such
a sympathy cannot take the place of a judgement of Blake's work.
When we know what prompted him to do what he did; even when
we find these promptings just; we have not shown that what he did
was also well done. And I do not think that it was always well done.
I think that Blake himself commonly made this mistake, of letting
his sympathy master his judgement. A sound sympathy drew Blake
to the Gothic; nevertheless, that rootless taste did him harm. For it
misled Blake, who could have faced the new, to give a false
prophetic worth to the fakes of Ossian and the Sublime.

> I Believe both Macpherson & Chatterton, that what they say
> is Ancient Is so.
> I own myself an admirer of Ossian equally with any other Poet
> whatever, Rowley & Chatterton also.   783

It made Blake, one of the few English painters who had not seen
the Italian paintings between which he chose with passion, also one
of the few who did not know the paintings shown by Count
Truchsess in 1803 for fakes.

> Suddenly, on the day after visiting the Truchsessian Gallery
> of pictures, I was again enlightened with the light I enjoyed in
> my youth, and which has for exactly twenty years been closed
> from me as by a door and by window-shutters.   852

And it is the taste in which Blake reasoned that because the sages
had beards, all bearded men are sages.

There is here a conflict in Blake between a strong invention and
an awe for random scraps of tradition, which is common in self-
taught men. It is marked in Blake's designs: the more marked, because they are the designs of an engraver. For though the Royal
Academy shut out the engravers from snobbery, the grounds which
they gave against them were reasonable. Engraving was, in large

part, a mechanical craft. It did not readily make a designer, it did not make a painter, either of Hogarth or of Blake. Hogarth could not force his invention beyond the harsh mechanics of caricature, because he believed that design is merely

> as clear a knowledge of the figure as a man who can write freely hath of the twenty-four letters of the alphabet and their infinite combinations.

These are matters of which I cannot claim to judge; I set down only my own likes. But it seems to me that Blake's designs are written in the same engraver's hand, and that it is at odds with the invention. The design peters out absent-mindedly in pattern; the figures are taken from standard prints and primers. The drawing is commonly flat and of surface only: the work of a man taught to make his pictures from those of others. Blake made a virtue of such impatience.

> To learn the Language of Art, 'Copy for Ever' is My Rule.   446
> Natural Objects always did & now do weaken, deaden & ob-
> literate Imagination in Me.   783

But it is the vague and mechanical workmanship which weakens, deadens, and at times obliterates Blake's great imagination.

For Blake was certainly the outstanding imaginative painter of his time. Everything that he was trying to do was new and vivid. At a time when painting had become a manner and a mannerism, Blake crowded his paintings with matter. It was not wholly a painter's matter; but neither was it a writer's matter: it was common to all that he did, the single and compact matter of a great imagination. And Blake knew how he wanted to put this matter. He knew that it needed a manner of its own: the sharp and sprightly outline of Michelangelo, solid but alive. Unhappily, I do not think that Blake could draw such an outline. He rightly scolded others for their puffy finish. 'These things that you call Finish'd are not Even Begun.' He justly saw that their shadowy Rubens outline was one with the vagueness and fear which haunted all their thought. But his own outline, although it is more fussy, does not seem to me more exact. Like Flaxman's, it commonly bounds only a surface; it does not hold the volume of the great Italian draughtsmen. There is a weight of space and volume in Blake's best designs.

But his best designs are few. More often he frankly does not know how to build a volume; his drawing is without skeleton, in clouds and jellies; and when he tries to give his figures the air of Michelangelo, the muscles with which he laces them are sham and grotesque. Blake traced the minute particulars of his vision.

> Without Minute Neatness of Execution The Sublime cannot
> Exist! Grandeur of Ideas is founded on Precision of Ideas.   457
> Singular & Particular Detail is the Foundation of the Sublime.   459

But he was seldom patient enough to turn his vision to the minute particulars of draughtsmanship.

I find in Blake's manner much of the *fauve*: his painting has the colour, the imaginative ease, and a hint of the surface tension of Matisse. It seldom has the depth of the Italian draughtsmen after which he laboured. For Michelangelo had not laboured after the ancients. His drawings had been discoveries: the discovery of a single order, the machine, in man and in the world. Their delight is that the muscle and the joint are of a piece with the rope and the pulley: as Blake sees himself at the end of his life, 'only bones & sinews, All strings & bobbins like a Weaver's Loom'. But Blake the craftsman was already at odds with the machine; and knew no other discovery to order his vision. His symbols began to divide like cells, his energy to go over itself like automatic writing, in vegetable chaos. Such a mind might have been at home in the more fluid mechanics of chemistry and of biology, which were then being discovered. It is perhaps a pity that Fuseli and Blake did not do more than their one plate for Erasmus Darwin's *The Botanic Garden*. Certainly their minds had no link with the static machinery which made the Industrial Revolution. And Fuseli's showy exercises in psychology were in flight from this machinery, no less than was Blake.

Fuseli knew the conflict between vivid matter and formless manner: he confessed that he could never paint up to what he saw. And Fuseli pointed sharply to this conflict in Blake, when he said that Blake was damned good to steal from. I think that Blake misunderstood this conflict. He thought that printers would not use his work because it was too harsh. But Wedgwood from his Etruria Works was just spreading the taste for the clear outline which

Flaxman and George Cumberland then, like Maillol and Matisse since, found apt for illustrations to Homer and Ovid. This mannered but sharp taste disliked Blake for the vague and automatic, the careless, the everyday in his drawing. It disliked them more in Blake's imagination. And Blake did let them master his imagination, until his vision itself became a medium's scribble.

THREE

This is not a book about Blake's designs; for I am not fitted to look at them with the pleasure and the care with which I read his writings. I do not set my judgement of Blake's pictures against the reader's, whether he thinks more or less highly of them than I do. I begin at the pictures only because, however we rate them, we cannot miss the strong grain of the everyday, the craftsman's manner, the handwriting in them. It is more striking, the more visionary Blake's pictures claim to be. It is most striking in the drawings which he made late in life for a dabbler in astrology, John Varley. For we cannot understand the inner vision throughout Blake's work unless we understand that from the outset it was Blake's everyday vision. All their lives Blake and his wife spoke of the dead whom they saw, not as conjured men, but as callers like the living. Blake's younger brother Robert went about the house after 1787 as he had done before, although it happened that he had died of consumption in that year. And Milton and God, when they called, said only what Blake had long laid down as his own belief. The news which these callers brought was canny.

> After dinner I ask'd Isaiah to favour the world with his lost works; he said— 154

Well, what would you have said in his place?

> He said none of equal value was lost. 154

The answer could not be bettered: 'Ezekiel said the same of his.'
   Blake's visions came in no heightened mood, but are his everyday moods. He looked at them with the insight with which he had looked at the face of the engraver William Wynne Ryland, when

his father had wanted to apprentice him to Ryland. He wrote of them with the energy, and with the extravagance, with which he had said of that face 'it looks as if he will live to be hanged'. Ryland was hanged in 1783, for forging bills of exchange. It may have been this story which made Blake all his life write Tyburn for a symbol of law and horror: Ryland's was the last hanging at that place, which is still marked at Marble Arch. But the story is not one of second sight but of insight. When Blake was taken to Ryland, some time in 1771, Ryland was at the end of his spendthrift years and his grand manner, and knew it; he was bankrupt before the end of the year. What Blake read in such a face, at such a time, was not a fate but a man.

> Every honest man is a Prophet; he utters his opinion both of private & public matters. Thus: If you go on So, the result is So. He never says, such a thing shall happen let you do what you will.
>
> 392

Nor did this insight work in Blake without error. It read forgery as a hanging crime in the face of Ryland. It failed to read murder in the face, debonair as Ryland's, of a man who befriended Blake late in life: Thomas Griffiths Wainewright, gossip, critic, painter, and poisoner. To be sure, Wainewright was only transported.

And as in his vision, so in his writings, Blake's prophetic gift is his everyday gift. Only so is it apt to give to his symbolic writings the name, the prophetic books; and then only because Blake himself fixed its workaday meaning. 'Every honest man is a Prophet; he utters his opinion both of private & public matters.' The symbolic manner of these books is large and rhetorical. But take it up anywhere; hold it at its most moving—

> How shall I flee, how shall I flee into the bower of Los?
> My feet are turned backward & my footsteps slide in clay: 335

it begins in the world which we know. The hint for this fine evangelical image comes from the hymns of Cowper; but we know precisely where Blake first wrote it. It was in a letter to his London patron Thomas Butts, when Blake was at Felpham in 1802.

> I am not ashamed, afraid, or averse to tell you what Ought to be Told: That I am under the direction of Messengers from

Heaven, Daily & Nightly; but the nature of such things is not, as some suppose, without trouble or care. Temptations are on the right hand & left; behind, the sea of time & space roars & follows swiftly; he who keeps not right onward is lost, & if our footsteps slide in clay, how can we do otherwise than fear & tremble? 812

To turn this into two lines of verse, Blake first transliterated it in eighty lines of constructed vision, which he sent to Butts later in the year. Painstakingly he there roared Los and Enitharmon—for 'Los is by mortals nam'd Time, Enitharmon is nam'd Space'—where once the sea of time and space had roared and followed swiftly. Prose, vision, and prophetic verse seem to speak of a less worldly life than ours. But turn to the beginning of the sounding passage which I have quoted:

My unhappiness has arisen from a source which, if explor'd too narrowly, might hurt my pecuniary circumstances, As my dependence is on Engraving at present, & particularly on the Engravings I have in hand for Mr H.: & I find on all hands great objections to my doing anything but the meer drudgery of business, & intimations that if I do not confine myself to this, I shall not live; this has always pursu'd me. You will understand by this the source of all my uneasiness. This from Johnson & Fuseli brought me down here, & this from Mr H. will bring me back again; for that I cannot live without doing my duty to lay up treasures in heaven is Certain & Determined. 812

Prose, vision, and prophetic verse are parts of a forthright debate, whether it is better to live at Felpham under Mr Hayley by engraving, or to starve alone in designing. And all come to the same choice: 'a determination which we have lately made, namely To leave This Place'.

FOUR

What is true of the matter of Blake's prophetic writings is true of their manner. The simplest comment on the other-worldly language of the letter from which I have quoted is Blake's own. Writing its debate more plainly to his older brother James, he added,

> This is the uneasiness I spoke of to Mr Butts, but I did not
> tell him so plain & wish you to keep it a secret & to burn this
> letter because it speaks so plain.   819

We mistake the language, and we mistake the meanings, of Blake's
prophetic books, if we forget the reasons which made Blake choose
and change that language. Blake chose his prophetic symbols because he found them apt to what he was saying; but he changed
their meanings, as the reasons for their aptness changed. Nothing
has hindered the understanding of Blake's prophetic books so much
as the wish to fix their symbols singly and steadily. These symbols
shift only within a well-marked framework: nevertheless, they do
shift, and they shift in order to remain apt to whatever actual
Blake then had in mind. The symbol of Los shifts from one of time
to one of energy, even within the narrow contexts from which I
have been quoting; and Satan changes completely.

This proliferation of meanings, unfolding from one stem, is
an orator's trick. And from the outset we must learn to read Blake's
prophetic manner, not as poetry, but as rhetoric. This is the harder,
because Blake also wrote poems; and most readers will feel as I do,
that his poems are more moving than his prophetic books. The
feeling is the mark of our common understanding, that Blake did
not write the two alike. But we must also understand that he was
not trying to write them alike. He was not trying to fix the sultry
symbolism of his prophetic books as he fixed the glass-clear images
of his poems. He was not trying to write the quick, lively, lifting
rhythms of his poems into his prophetic books. Blake was a bold
and sensitive inventor of rhythms all his life; all his life he wrote
poems and prophetic books together; yet he never took the slack
rhythms and the loose phrasing, which he also invented, outside
his prophetic books. He held them to their place, because only in
that place did they fulfil their purpose.

> Why stand we here trembling around
> Calling on God for help, and not ourselves, in whom God
>   dwells,
> Stretching a hand to save the falling Man? are we not Four
> Beholding Albion upon the Precipice ready to fall into Non-
>   Entity?   672

> All you my Friends & Brothers, all you my beloved Com-
>   panions,
> Have you also caught the infection of Sin & stern Re-
>   pentance?
> I see Disease arise upon you! yet speak to me and give
> Me some comfort! why do you all stand silent?   673

Of course these lines, with their marked hortative rhythm and purpose, come from a prophetic book. And they come from a book
whose orator's manner Blake avowed, *Jerusalem*.

> When this Verse was first dictated to me, I consider'd a
> Monotonous Cadence, like that used by Milton & Shakspeare
> & all writers of English Blank Verse, derived from the modern
> bondage of Rhyming, to be a necessary and indispensible part
> of Verse. But I soon found that in the mouth of a true Orator
> such monotony was not only awkward, but as much a bondage
> as rhyme itself.   621

But Blake, like Dryden before him, found rhyme a bondage only
when he was writing rhetoric.

Rhetoric is an extravagant manner; but it remains a manner of
the everyday. It uses imagery to give to everyday speech, not depth
and not precision, but energy. And energy becomes the keyword to
Blake's prophetic books: 'Energy is Eternal Delight.' The same
preface To *the Public* from which I have quoted, set before *Jerusalem*, underlines the everyday and the energetic in the book.

> I pretend not to holiness: yet I pretend to love, to see, to
> converse with daily as man with man, & the more to have an
> interest in the Friend of Sinners. Therefore, [dear] Reader,
> [forgive] what you do not approve, & [love] me for this ener-
> getic exertion of my talent.   621

These words are also Blake's answer to those who seek in his
prophetic books only the secret system. They show that Blake
himself knew that, at bottom, his symbolism is held together only
by his energy and his imaginative insight. For Blake was not trying
to puzzle out a secret or a system. He was trying to make men give
up systems, rationalist and religious alike. And he was trying 'to
converse with daily as man with man'.

FIVE

I do not wish to belittle those who have found Blake's mysticism more absorbing than they have found Blake. Of course there have been cranks, in Blake's lifetime and since, who have merely forced their own system into Blake; but that temper is not the monopoly of mystics. There have been painstaking readers who have traced Blake's symbols to Swedenborg, to Boehme, to the Gnostics, and to the Cabbala; and we are indebted to them. I myself, whose reading in these matters does not go beyond the Bible and some Jewish mystics, have been astonished to find how readily he took over any symbol which he found vaguely to his purpose. Blake's largest source seems to me to have been *Revelation*, alike for such prose as his notes to Watson's *Apology for the Bible* and such verse as *The Book of Urizen*. And there is a welter of symbols in Blake which goes back, by whatever steps, to the Cabbala: his Four States, his Trees, his Spectre and Emanation, his Divine Image, his Seven Eyes, his 'Jerusalem in every Man'. The Cabbala has a hint of Blake's strikingly modern dialectic of Contraries and Progression. It has the geography of his *Milton*. Even the oddly closed geometry of Blake's world may be that of the Cabbalistic spheres, if I understand them rightly; and is kin to the Gnostic spiral which Blake drew in *Jacob's Ladder*, and to such symbols as the snake-ring.

We can certainly enlarge this list a hundredfold; we can show that its sources are ten times as many, and ten times more scattered. Yet we shall then have shown, more certainly, that these formal likenesses tell us little of Blake's thought. For the more symbols we find Blake to have picked up, and the more random their sources, the plainer it becomes that he took them less by choice than from habit. All these symbols were alike to Blake, because all were to him shadows of the same mystery. The mystery is that the one and the many are parts, each of the other; that in the beginning is the end, and that the centre meets the circumference. To hold together two such poles, in whatever form—the subject with the object, the ego with the id, man with society—this is the oneness for which the mystic strives. But just this is the aim, not of one mystic, but of all.

All Blake's symbols link the one with the many, inside with outside,
the face with the mask. All Blake's thought then sets itself the
mystic's aim; but we have still to ask, How does it reach its aim?
We have still to look at his symbols, not for what they have in
common with those of all mystics, but for what they do not.

There is no doubt what makes Blake's mysticism uncommon:
alone among such other-worldly thinkers, he founded it on a harsh
understanding of the actual. Blake made a symbolism of his own in
giving to the states of man the names of cities. But the reader who
wants to map these states must understand the worldly meaning of
each name.

> Benevolent Bath,
> Bath who is Legions; he is the Seventh, the physician and
> The poisoner, the best and worst in Heaven and Hell.   668

The double symbol here, and the joining of the inner and outer
spheres: these are the commonplaces of mysticism. There is one
thing which is uncommon; and it is the one thing which Blake put
there by choice: the name Bath. Only the vivid, shrewd mind of
Blake could have made eighteenth-century Bath, place of healing
and of corruption at once, a symbol in the timeless dualism of the
mystic.

There is a history to every name in Blake's lists.

> In Tyre & Sidon I saw Baal & Ashtaroth: In Moab Chemosh:
> In Ammon Molech, loud his Furnaces rage among the Wheels
> Of Og, & pealing loud the cries of the Victims of Fire,
> And pale his Priestesses infolded in Veils of Pestilence
>   border'd .
> With War, Woven in Looms of Tyre & Sidon by beautiful
>   Ashtaroth:
> In Palestine Dagon, Sea Monster, worship'd o'er the Sea:
> Thammuz in Lebanon & Rimmon in Damascus curtain'd:
> Osiris, Isis, Orus in Egypt, dark their Tabernacles on Nile
> Floating with solemn songs & on the Lakes of Egypt nightly
> With pomp even till morning break & Osiris appear in the
>   sky:
> But Belial of Sodom & Gomorrha, obscure Demon of Bribes
> And secret Assasinations, not worship'd nor ador'd, but
> With a finger on the lips & the back turn'd to the light:

D

And Saturn, Jove & Rhea of the Isles of the Sea remote.
These Twelve Gods are the Twelve Spectre Sons of the
    Druid Albion.   528

But the history of these names is not to be found in books of comparative religion. The reader who thumbs after these gods will find it hard to count them so as to make just twelve; and he will find little else. The list comes alive only in its lightning rhetorical images, each seen with fresh insight and each charged with fresh hatred. Blake lingered on three of these images: why these three? Why had Blake come to hear in the spectral Albion the man-burning furnaces of Moloch and the looms of Tyre and Sidon weaving war? Why did he come back with tender loathing, here and elsewhere, to the poisoned Cleopatra image of Egypt, its 'night of delicious songs', 'the night of prosperity & wantonness'? And most swiftly seen, most frighteningly held of all: why did Blake mark in his Albion the figure of the spy and censor, the *agent provocateur*?

> Belial of Sodom & Gomorrha, obscure Demon of Bribes
> And secret Assasinations, not worship'd nor ador'd, but
> With a finger on the lips & the back turn'd to the light.   528

These questions take us to the base of Blake's thought. In their answer lies the understanding, not of these fifteen lines alone, but of Blake's prophetic books. This is to look beyond their system, the formal grammar of Blake's thought, into its language.

S I X

Of course, the largest puzzles in Blake have always been the puzzles of his shifting language. When Blake from Felpham called Butts the 'Dear Friend of My Angels', Butts answered,

> I cannot immediately determine whether or no I am dignified by the Title you have graciously conferred on me. You cannot but recollect the difficulties that have unceasingly arisen to prevent my discerning whether your Angels are black, white, or grey.

This is heavy fun, but it is shrewd fun. And it is the ground on which good readers of the time, Wordsworth, Coleridge, Lamb, found Blake maddening and called him mad. It is the ground on which Blake's own friends thought him wilfully awkward. They did not doubt the great sweep of his thought; Wordsworth did not miss that when he found 'something in the madness of this man which interests me more than the sanity of Lord Byron and Walter Scott'. And they did not doubt that Blake spoke what he thought. But they doubted whether his language, however like theirs, was the same as theirs. And unless Blake spoke their language, could he speak to them? Unless he hit the pitch of their ear, could he be said even to be thinking aloud? Were Blake's writings less aimless than those vast harangues, ten, twelve, sixteen hours together, in which George III's porphyria foamed into madness in 1788?

Such puzzles, however, were not set by Blake alone. Chatterton and Wordsworth also strained against their readers' language; and Cowper and John Clare went mad. The rhetoric of the Wesleyan revival and of Burke became formless in hysteria. The oddities of Blake, in word and act, belong to this larger context. Certainly the men who thought Blake mad were wrong; but they were not silly. Each kind of madness is a distortion of privacy, at its boundary with the social world. The privacy of the mad may collapse inward like Cowper's, or explode outward like Burke's; but it does so under the strain of that world. The men of Blake's day felt the strain in him, because they feared it in themselves. William Wordsworth held it anxiously within his language, until all thought withered in him. But Dorothy Wordsworth went mad. Blake knew what discontent made him and others pit their language against the world's, and drove them to madness 'as a refuge from unbelief'.

> There are States in which all Visionary Men are accounted
> Mad Men; such are Greece & Rome: Such is Empire or Tax. 777

The men of Blake's day who called him mad were less glib than others who have since called him sane. For they did not miss the larger context of his discontent.

The context of that age of rhetoric and madness is now less well known than is Blake. It is ironic that it is easier to fix, say George

Crabbe and William Wilberforce, by taking bearings from Blake, than to fix Blake from them. Nevertheless, the aim to which I have held in what follows is the understanding of Blake alone. Because his context is large, I have had to be painstaking. I ask the patience of those readers who are as precise as I have tried to be with the American war, the French Revolution and wars, and the towering background of the Industrial Revolution. Blake did not merely live through these: he lived them, in his own impersonal life; and he lived them into his prophetic books. The life of Blake, and his thought, are not to be coaxed from the few letters which he wrote from Felpham to his London friends, and from London while he still had friends at Felpham. They are there, for all to read, in the history of his time; in the names of Pitt, of Paine, and of Napoleon; in the hopes of rationalists, and in the despair of craftsmen. Until we know these, we shall not understand Blake's poems, we shall not understand his thought, because we shall not speak his language.

Yet when we speak Blake's language, shall we needs understand his meaning? Is it apt, in reading Blake's poems, to give them a meaning? For, is there a meaning to give? A. E. Housman, who put Blake higher among poets than I do, held that

> Blake's meaning is often unimportant or virtually non-existent, so that we can listen with all our hearing to his celestial tune.

I take it that Housman was not saying that Blake himself wrote without a meaning. For, however sagely critics say that poems are made of sounds and rhythms, poets robustly go on making them of words; and can no more speak the word without its meaning than without its sound. Certainly poems make uncommonly much of their tune. Certainly, if you choose to think of other arts, poems are made with words as pictures are painted with colours. But pictures are painted with colours: they do not paint colours. They paint surfaces and volumes, they order shapes and masses, they use the knowledge of what colours do to make a meaning. So sound, rhythm, tune, words in the poem make a meaning; so these in each of his poems make a meaning for the poet's whole work; and the work in turn enriches each of its parts. I hope that this book leaves no doubt that Blake put a meaning into his life's work.

What I take Housman to have been pointing to is the thin privacy, the glimpse of madness in Blake's poems, which make it seem easy to read them without a meaning. Unhappily, it is no easier to read than to write without a meaning; and the reader who does not catch Blake's meaning has commonly already put in his own. There is a poem in *A Shropshire Lad* which begins,

> Farewell to barn and stack and tree,
>   Farewell to Severn shore.
> Terence, look your last at me,
>   For I come home no more.
>
> The sun burns on the half-mown hill,
>   By now the blood is dried;
> And Maurice amongst the hay lies still
>   And my knife is in his side.
>
> My mother thinks us long away;
>   'Tis time the field were mown.
> She had two sons at rising day,
>   To-night she'll be alone.

I think that when Housman wrote this poem, his mind unawares was touched off by an image from Blake:

> The brother & the brother bathe in blood upon the Severn,
> The Maiden weeping by. The father & the mother with
> The Maiden's father & her mother fainting over the body,
> And the Young Man, the Murderer, fleeing over the
>   mountains.   281

If I am right, Housman's poem shows that he read his own outlook into Blake: in what he left out, no less than in what he took.

Blake's poems can be read with very simple meanings. It shows the depth of Blake's mind that, though he did not think of them so, they can be so read. And the reader who wants to come back at last to Blake's poems, as I do, is right to ask, Will all this stumbling over Pitt and the prophetic books enrich the meaning? He is right to ask what knowledge and what pleasure he will gain, at such pains, to enlarge the pleasures of sound, of rhythm, and of tune, the simple happiness and sadness, the springing pattern and the conjured moods, which are uppermost in Blake's poems. But he must beware of asking only because he wishes to hold to his own meanings. He must beware of choosing his own meanings in place of Blake's, merely because he knows his to be less searching. There is no doubt that Blake's poems meant more to him than they can do to any one of his readers. There is no doubt that they held for him compactly the meanings for which he fumbled in the rhetoric of the prophetic books. We need not ask, therefore, whether the prophetic books are apt to Blake's poems. They are. But we may ask whether they are apt enough to repay these pains.

SEVEN

The most forthright answer to this question is that which Swinburne gave.

> What is true of all poets and artists worth judging is especially true of him: that critics who attempt to judge him piecemeal do not in effect judge him at all, but some one quite different from him, and some one (to any serious student) probably more inexplicable than the real man.

The word which I would stress here is 'inexplicable'. For surely the reader of Blake's poems must ask himself, why Blake did not write his prophetic books like them. Why is the imagery of the prophetic books smoky and violent where that of the poems is lucid? Why is the language of the prophetic books fluid and secretive, commonplace yet wilful, when the poems speak with open face? Why did that poetic face, *The Divine Image*, choose to put on its prophetic mask?

These questions have hardly been put. So many have asked, How? of the prophetic books, that few have asked the blunter question, Why? This, however, is my question. And this has taken me away from the source books, to the living sources of Blake's language. It is a long journey for one like myself, who finds the worth of Blake at last in his poems. But it is the journey of Blake's own Traveller; and like him, I know at the end that the beginning has been enriched by it. Having tried to understand the whole of Blake, I have found it shining back into every part. This is my belief, and I hope to make it the reader's. It was certainly Blake's belief.

But no such understanding works of itself. When we have learnt Blake's language, we have still to judge what he said with it. When we have stripped the mask, we have still to judge the face; and it is an act of judgement, even to find them one. What follows is not written because it makes judgement needless, but because without it judgement is helpless. The world in which Blake lived stands stark in the *Songs of Experience*; but it did not of itself make the *Songs of Experience*; and it certainly does not make them good or bad. Yet that world may have made the *Songs of Experience* less round than the *Songs of Innocence*. Perhaps such a book as this tells us about the things which Blake did greatly, only that they were not burdened by the misery which made him do other things ill. It is not a judgement of what is great, and it does not tell us how the great is made. It tells us how a world can cripple what should have been great.

THE SEDITIOUS WRITINGS

Trade

The year 1757, in which Blake was born, was a year of dearth. So scarce was corn that Parliament forbade its use in the making of spirits. Such an act had not been spoken of for a hundred years and more. For a hundred years and more, England had commonly grown more corn than she used; and for most of this time, Governments had paid a bounty for its export. But from 1757, throughout Blake's life, the years of dearth grew common. In 1795 the younger Pitt was trying to eke out a war budget by taxing those who powdered their hair a guinea a head. But that·year flour was so scarce that he had to forbid its use in hair-powder. The four-pound loaf had cost 3d. before the dearths; in 1801 it reached the famine price of 1s. 10d. When Blake died, in 1827, landowners no longer pressed for a bounty on the export of corn. They had carried the Corn Laws against a rioting country a dozen years before Blake's death, and they held to them for nearly twenty years after it. But these laws took protection no farther than to restrict the import of corn.

England then ceased to grow enough corn for her needs during Blake's lifetime. It is one of a web of changes, no single one of them cause and no one of them effect, whose strands cross over and over these seventy years. It is certainly linked with the growth of population; with thirty-five years of war, piracy, and blockade; with mounting debts, taxes, and poor-rates; with the rise in prices, and with economic *let be*. And these in turn are linked with the enlargement of factory industry and of finished exports; with the

43

enclosure of common land; with the decay of smallholders and craftsmen, and the use of unskilled workers; with shifts in political power and loyalty, and with a changing social outlook. This is the web, bewildering in detail and overwhelming in the large, which goes by the name of the Industrial Revolution.

The industrial changes, which this name underlines, were indeed the most far-reaching of all: they were a revolution. But we must read the name strictly; this was an industrial revolution: it did not revolutionize England, but industry. The revolution came to an England whose wealth was made in cottages, and it moved the sources of wealth to factories. But the wealth throughout was founded in a simple machine industry. At bottom, the revolution was no more than a powerful way of drawing this industry together. England did not become an industrial country at the end of the eighteenth century; for she was an industrial country long before. When Blake was born, her exports had already reached £15,000,000 a year, having doubled since the beginning of the century. The Industrial Revolution could not quite treble this sum before the century ended. And a hundred years before Blake, England had been enlarging her export trade by very modern means. She had provoked war against Holland in 1665, designedly in order to ruin the Dutch trade with Africa.

Nevertheless the Industrial Revolution did end an age. At its birth, and Blake's, there died an order of society as well as of industry. The age of the Whigs, that Indian summer of village industry, was ended. It had been the last age built on England's age-old monopoly: the great range of her wools, and the crafts of working them all. The woollen cloth had been a treasure more plentiful than gold, and as marketable and current the world over. With this had been paid the larger world trade which, for a hundred years before Blake was born, had been making England greater than the empires of Spain and France, and richer than the carrying trade of Holland. England's empire was begun on the bottom of village industry; on this rested her liberal dissenters, her society of moneyed men, her great Whig houses. And the staple of this industry held its own for some time still. To the end of the eighteenth century, the woollen cloth made up one-third of England's exports, and of her whole output. But cotton,

he new staple of factory industry, was gaining fast; and overtook
wool as soon as the century turned. Thirty years before Blake was
born, Defoe had held up the weavers of the West Riding wool
country as the models of industry, and the pride of society. But
before Blake died, a Parliamentary Committee found that hand-
loom weavers of cotton were earning 6s. 4d. a week. The bottom
had gone from village industry.

TWO

The masters of village industry had not been owners but merchants.
These merchants had long been putting out their own raw stuffs
to be worked. And they had begun to take the craftsman's tools in
pawn, before Blake was born. Yet it is fair to think of the village
worker of that age as commonly owning his tools, and as often owning his raw stuffs, at least in law. He made hats and watches, linen
and small-arms, he made silk in Spitalfields and stockings in Nottingham, Manchester cotton pieces and Birmingham nails: and
he still made them largely at his own risk. Cloth was still made
by men whose capital was a loom and perhaps a week's wool, and
whose labour was their own and their families'. Some of these
men still took cloth to market, and some great clothiers still bought
it there; in law at least, the men bought another week's wool, and
went back to their weaving. Growing richer, such men might buy
two or three looms, and hire hands to work them; they might put
out wool to be spun in other villages; but they remained well-to-do
master workmen, the men whose praise fills Defoe; and they seldom
became clothiers. And factory industry did not begin from the
growth of these men, but from their mortgaging step by step to
the merchant adventurers or their middlemen. Where a factory
industry had been set up earlier, as in the West Country, it was
in fact falling into decay.

Village industry was thus the base for a society of trade, paid
in ready money. At bottom the changes through which Blake lived
were from village to factory industry; at the top they were from
a society of money to one of capital. Money was invested before
Blake was born; but it was seldom invested as industrial capital;
because there were few industries whose plant was large enough

to need share capital. There were a few such industries: mining
shipbuilding, the making of glass and metals; and the adventurer
in these had early formed some kinds of joint-stock companie
But outside these few, there was no industrial plant; and join
stock companies and share capital were almost unknown. Whe
Blake was born there was a money market for trade; there wer
banks and insurance companies; but trade was the buying an
selling, not the making of goods. Only in Blake's lifetime did th
merchants fall back before the new masters of factory industry
Arkwright and Wilkinson, the Peels and the Wedgwoods. An
men who lived through the change, men in Government as well a
men in the street, hardly understood that it was a change. The
went on thinking of the rich of their society as traders who ha
merely strayed into industry. Blake saw more deeply than othe
into the ways of industrial combination and monopoly. But t
the end of his life he spoke of them as 'the Arts of Trading Con
bination' and

> the interest of the Monopolizing Trader who Manufactures
> Art by the Hands of Ignorant Journeymen till at length
> Christian Charity is held out as a Motive to encourage a
> Blockhead, & he is Counted the Greatest Genius who can
> sell a Good-for-Nothing Commodity for a Great Price.   59

What word but Trader could Blake use, at a time when the nam
Manufacturer was still given, literally, to the handworker, as com
monly as to the employer of factory hands?

The merchant of the Whig age had, of course, ranged far beyon
the trade in English manufactures. This trade had given hin
money, ships, and power; and had thus given him the means to
trade in the goods of all countries. He had used these means to
build a world trade, above all in the raw stuffs of America and th
manufactures of India. Bristol and Liverpool had grown grea
by this trade, long before the Shropshire ironmasters and th
Lancashire drapers became the masters of English industry. Bu
whether the goods which the merchant shipped were English o
foreign, his was a short-term money speculation, not a long-term
capital investment. He gambled against the hazards of war, piracy
and shipwreck; and since he smuggled quite half his goods, h

ambled against those Customs officers whom he did not buy. And
e looked for the dividends of the gambler rather than the in-
estor.

THREE

The gaming-house, the race-course, the underwriter's office, and
he market in trading stocks all grew up in the moneyed society
of the early eighteenth century. The lottery became the common
means of raising public money, for taxes, for the building of Westminster Bridge, for the founding of the British Museum. John Gay,
who was too proud to take the sinecure of Gentleman Usher to a
princess, was not ashamed to hold that of Commissioner of the
State Lottery. Men so prim as Addison, and so rich as Fox's father,
won large lottery prizes. For a merchant society risks its money
without the backing which industrial plant gives, and makes it without the checks which that sets. It gambles for its livelihood
without squeamishness: in trade, in money, in patronage, and in
bribery. The tongue-tied unhappiness which falls on Blake whenever he speaks of money shows the striking change which the
Industrial Revolution worked here. Edward Young had thought
it no shame to write to a Whig Prime Minister in 1726,

> My breast, O Walpole, glows with grateful fire.
> The streams of royal bounty, turn'd by thee,
> Refresh the dry domains of poesy.

Put this beside the embarrassment with which Blake in 1804 asks
Hayley to pay him for his work:

> I must now tell my wants, & beg the favour of some more of
> the needful: 851

we are in another society.

   The men of Young's society fought for their money as frankly
as they begged. They had begun the Whig age in 1688 by turning
out James II, and making William III king; and they set themselves to make money a Whig monopoly. They founded the Bank
of England, and the Tory squires failed to found a land bank
against it. They founded a new East India Company, and the

Tory squires failed to hold the older company against them. A Tory Government in 1711 had challenged them, by floating a loan conversion through the South Sea Company, which it founded for that end. But when this company in 1720 tried spectacularly to corner the money market, the Bank and the East India Company broke it. Thereafter, the City and the great Whig houses, the Percys, the Cavendishes, the Russells, the Howards, ruled unchallenged. Swift might go on pouring out his bitter dignity, that he

> abominated that scheme of politics (now about thirty years old) of setting up a moneyed interest in opposition to the landed.
>
> It is the Folly of too many, to mistake the Eccho of a *London* Coffee-house for the Voice of the Kingdom. The City Coffee-houses have been for some Years filled with People, whose Fortunes depend upon the *Bank, East-India,* or some other Stock: Every new Fund to these, is like a new Mortgage to an Usurer, whose Compassion for a young Heir is exactly the same with that of a Stockjobber to the Landed Gentry.

But the landed gentry, the little Tory squires for whom Swift spoke, were no longer a power. The large landowners in the House of Lords had long been linked to the wool and other trades, and shared the money market. They were the very men who had brought William III to England. When Swift wrote, they were doubling their wealth in the growing corn market. And they were staunch in the Whig connexion. Pope might go on raging against

> London's voice: 'Get Mony, Mony still!
> And then let Virtue follow, if she will':

the voice which

> whispers, 'Be but Great,
> With Praise or Infamy, leave that to fate;
> Get Place and Wealth, if possible, with Grace;
> If not, by any means get Wealth and Place.'

He might see the whole society fawn on political jobbery:

> See thronging Millions to the Pagod run,
> And offer Country, Parent, Wife, or Son!

> Hear her black Trumpet thro' the Land proclaim,
> That 'Not to be corrupted is the Shame'.

But he was so urgent, only because the corruption was so able. The Whig connexion had the means to bribe, and it knew whom to bribe. It calmly went on buying the Opposition. It had made a society, compact of the large holdings of trade and land, in the single interest of money. And whatever the cost, it defended it.

FOUR

The cost was high. William III had brought John Locke with him from Holland, and had put him into the Court of Appeals and the Board of Trade, to lay down the ends of Whig society.

> The great and chief end, therefore, of men's uniting into
> commonwealths, and putting themselves under government,
> is the preservation of their property.

It is fair to add that Locke used the word 'property' to mean life and freedom as well as wealth: yet that usage, of that word, is itself revealing. When Locke wrote, in 1690, there were fewer than fifty hanging crimes. By the time that Blake was a boy, about 1767, Sir William Blackstone's *Commentaries on the Laws of England* counted about a hundred and fifty; and the number was still growing. Within another ten years, Adam Smith put Locke's point with no fine usage.

> The affluence of the rich excites the indignation of the poor,
> who are often both driven by want and prompted by envy
> to invade their possessions. It is only under the shelter of the
> civil magistrate that the owner of that valuable property
> which is acquired by the labour of many years, or perhaps of
> many successive generations, can sleep a single night in se-
> curity.

Blake saw truly when he came to use Locke's name as a byword for a self-willed society of poverty, and for

> the wretched State of the Arts in this Country & in Europe,
> originating in the wretched State of Political Science, which
> is the Science of Sciences.   600

E

For political science and its law did not hang for crimes against the body, such as attempted murder. They did not hang for what were thought to be crimes against the spirit, such as witchcraft: in spite of Blackstone and the Bible, that had ceased to be a crime in 1736. Most of the new hanging crimes were crimes against wealth. Men were hanged for stealing forty shillings' worth of goods from a house, or five shillings' worth from a shop. They were hanged if they had not been seen to steal; they were not hanged if the theft had been witnessed. There were murderers whom it was found simpler to hang for burglary, and burglars whom it was simpler to hang for cutting down a tree. Wainewright was transported not for his murders but for forgery: the forgery, of course, was on one of the two great monopolies, the Bank of England, as Ryland's had been on the other, the East India Company. We may judge how the law chose between Locke's meanings of property, from the crimes of two men who were whipped round Covent Garden while Blake was an apprentice: the one for raping his niece, the other for stealing a bunch of radishes. The law was not merely savage, for lack of a police force; it was vicious, because it was irresponsible.

Savagery and irresponsibility are the stamp of the town life of that age. It was not easy for a man to move about the country. The Elizabethan Poor Law held with little change long after Blake was born; and it gave a man the right to relief only in the parish where he had settlement. Country parishes would spend five, ten, twenty pounds to forestall his settlement, lest he fall on the rates at some time. Only a bold, a foolhardy, or a desperate man would risk losing the right to relief, which was to him unemployment insurance, health insurance, and old-age pension in one. And such men drifted to the crowded parishes whose bumbles were too busy to pester them: the towns. The thief and the beggar drifted into town; but so did the honest man, hopeful or desperate; and once there, he often found no choice but to turn either thief or beggar. The town had little other work to offer him.

For the town as we now know it is built round factory industries. But the industries of that time were scattered through such groups of villages as Manchester, Birmingham, and the Five Towns then were. The eighteenth-century town lived by trade. It housed some craftsmen, who tried to guard their skill and their status carefully.

But the bulk of its poor lived by casual work. The casual worker, English or often Irish, might earn much one day and nothing the next; because he lived uncertainly, he squandered the much on whores and publicans: in short, the eighteenth-century town lived like the trade town of to-day, the port. The largest towns of the time, London, Bristol, Liverpool, Glasgow, and Dublin, were in fact ports. Their squalor was the squalor of the slums and stews of Marseilles. They were overcrowded: for town building to house the poor, who had little to do there, was for long unlawful. They were, of course, unwholesome, although it is not certain that they were more unwholesome than the cottages of the country poor. They were riotous and dangerous, the home of the pimp and the pickpocket, the sharper, the footpad, and the gangster: even the highwayman was a London, not a country pest. They lived from hand to mouth, by their wits. And they snatched their happiness in the stupor of gin. Nothing tells so frighteningly the misery of the poor in the towns as the rise of gin drinking, until the cheap raw spirit became less a drug than an infection. Seventy years before Blake's birth England had been drinking about half a million gallons of spirits a year. When Blake was born, she was drinking nearly eight million gallons a year: about a gallon each man, woman, and child. Three Acts of Parliament had not halted the evil; it fell back only in face of the dearths of corn. And in the year of his death Blake could still write, as a bitter pun about the Holy Ghost,

> Spirits are Lawful, but not Ghosts; especially Royal Gin is
> Lawful Spirit.   787

Into this thieves' kitchen, the London still of Hogarth of *A Rake's Progress* and *Gin Lane*, William Blake was born. Here the rich and the poor still gambled together; and Gay had wondered which aped the vices of the other. Here the men who fought their way up never lost the scars and the fears of their past. Samuel Johnson when he had £300 a year still tore at his food like a dog. But Johnson had lived like a dog; he had known his friend Richard Savage die like a dog. The men who rose dared not look at their money too closely. Johnson's £300 was a pension from George III, whose right to the Crown Johnson denied; and Johnson had taken it, seven years after his dictionary had defined a pension as

'pay given to a state hireling for treason to his country'. Those who
fell gambled even in the dock. Since punishment was savage,
unequal, and random, juries at times were loth to convict: Would
they rate the theft at more than five shillings, or less? Would they
call a bank-note money or paper? If the gambler lost, the crowd
would turn out for him in gentlemanly acknowledgement; and he,
in gentlemanly acknowledgement, sometimes hanged fairly cheer-
fully. For the crowd which made a legend of the sordid lives of
gunmen was speaking its sympathy with all that was reckless,
lawless, and anti-social. Gay, in *The Beggar's Opera*, and Henry
Fielding had found the story of the receiver Jonathan Wild, who
was hanged in 1725, an apt satire on their Governments. But if the
crowd read, it read the story as Defoe told it; and found it more
terribly apt to the double dealing of a whole society. Its heroes
spoke the gambler's contempt for a society of cheats. When
Blake was a young man the crowd still gathered at *The Dog and
Duck* near St George's Fields to see the highwaymen set off and

> the flashy women come out to take leave of the thieves at
> dusk and wish them success.

FIVE

Yet it was a society; and when Blake was born it could still flower
richly. The elder Pitt had become Prime Minister in that year.
Within four years he had broken the imperial power of France,
fear of which had shaped Whig Policy for seventy years in war
and peace. While Frederick the Great marched and counter-
marched like another Marlborough to hold France in Europe,
Pitt took the hope of Indian empire from her at Plassey in 1757;
won her Canadian empire at Quebec in 1759; and broke her sea
power in two battles in the West Indies, in 1759 and 1761. Vast
markets were opened to England: at the peace of 1763 she rated
the untapped market of Canada higher than the spice islands of
the West Indies. A world lay conquered for her trade; a greater
Whig age seemed about to begin. The trade came, but the Whigs
went. For in 1760 a Tory and a High Churchman, George III, had
become by the Grace of God King, Defender of the Faith. In

1761 Pitt resigned. About this time the child Blake saw his first vision of God, and screamed.

Self-willed, narrow, patient, dull, and unbelievably mulish, George III was not a man who should make history. Nor is it likely that he made it. He pressed from the beginning of his reign the Tory policy which England took up thirty years later. But England did not take up this policy because it was his. George III and his policy were both disliked; and he went on being disliked after the policy became common. Larger fears made that Tory reaction country-wide, from the time of the French Revolution in 1789: fear of the unseen but haunting mass of the poor which the Industrial Revolution and the enclosures were making. George III was merely the symbol of Toryism: at most, a chance first fruit of reaction.

When George III became king, the Young Pretender was sullenly drinking himself to death. But George III set out to remake a Toryism more Stuart than his. He set himself to be a king: and his notion of kingship was to be free of the interests which made England, whatever they might be. This was not because he thought himself fitted to rule. He thought, and said, that he would 'make but a very poor and despicable figure'; and it is one of his few sound judgements. He distrusted himself, and dared not meet statesmen of power and ability lest he 'be shackled by those desperate men'. He enlarged these jealous fears to a hysteria which faced every trifling change with the will, in a cold sweat, that

> whilst any ten men in the Kingdom will stand by me, I will not give myself up to bondage.

This is a temper to pity, and to smile at. But it remained the temper of his grand-daughter, more than a hundred years later, firm that

> She will sooner *abdicate* than send for or have *any communication* with *that half-mad firebrand* who would soon ruin everything and be a *Dictator*.

Queen Victoria wrote this in 1880 about Gladstone. And it leaves no doubt that George III's Toryism had little to do with the larger fears which came to unite owners later in his reign. The causes of fear were not yet over the horizon, even during the American war from 1775, when George III wrote and rewrote his abdications. But England was ruled by the Toryism of fear; and soon Blake would see

> Infinite London's awful spires cast a dreadful cold
> Even on rational things beneath and from the palace walls
> Around Saint James's, chill & heavy, even to the city gate.   205

> The King of England looking westward trembles at the vision. 197

To drive the Whigs from public life, George III did not scruple to corrupt that life more openly than they had dared. The Secret Service fund bought votes for the King's Friends at elections. Ireland was taxed to death for sinecures in his gift. In his lifetime George III doubled the shrinking House of Lords, which hitherto had counted fewer than two hundred peers: and made it what John Wilkes foretold, the Dead Weight of the Constitution. Designedly, George III filled his Governments with weak and anxious men. Within three years he had embroiled them with Wilkes, for no better reason than that Wilkes was a tool of the elder Pitt. Although Wilkes might have been bought cheaply in 1765, George III carried on the quarrel, always in the wrong, until Wilkes became spokesman for the whole City interest. By 1774 Wilkes was Lord Mayor of London, and had been elected to Parliament five times by Middlesex, in face of four unlawful expulsions. He at once attacked the threatened war against America on behalf of the City and of the Americans, who both petitioned through him. We can trace the singleness of these liberal trading interests in that Wilkes and Benjamin Franklin, then in London on behalf of the Americans, were both Freemasons. Blake took some of his symbolism from Freemasonry.

SIX

Blake grew to be a man during the American war, from 1775 to 1783. The causes of this war were manifold. The American colonies could not have been held for ever under laws which forbade them all trade but with England; Ireland also rebelled against such laws in time. The colonies could not have been forbidden for ever to manufacture from their own raw stuffs. They could not be denied for ever a greater share in their local governments. They wanted freedom to move into newly conquered French lands. And freed of a French threat, they wanted above all to be let be. Yet it is not certain that these wishes need have become pressing in George III's long reign, had not his Ministries of None of the Talents chosen to repress them.

The Ministers indeed were fairly helpless. The elder Pitt had won an empire; but they still had to pay for the victory, in a time of dearths, slump, and rising prices. They were not simply prompted by budget needs; yet these needs made a show of reasonableness for acts which were foolish. They were taking the Tory line in every slump: to retrench, and to shift the burden of upkeep elsewhere. And since they did not understand the Whig 'clamour of trade, of the merchants, and of the manufacturing towns', that slumps can be eased only by easing trade, they turned their colonial policy into a party fight.

They began by trying, in 1764, to check American smuggling to and from the French West Indies. This smuggling had always been unlawful. But without it, the trading laws were unworkable. The West Indies had become the clearing house for American export of sugar, tobacco, timber, and other raw stuffs, and for the import of manufactures and of slaves. Usage and need had made a right of this smuggling, as open as England's unlawful right to smuggle to Spanish South America. It was only twenty-five years since England had gone to war with Spain to uphold her right.

Where both sides were thus righteous and ill at ease, both looked for a better quarrel in trifles. They quarrelled over petty taxes. Having withdrawn some, the Ministers made a show of dignity with others; and the Americans saw in them the show of spite. In 1772 the slump broke many English banks and houses, among them the East India Company. The Government in effect took India from the Company; and in exchange allowed it to take tea to America without taxing it in England. It was a smaller trifle than others, and likely to harm no one but Boston holders of stocks of dear tea. But it was a break with the vexed trading laws, made not on behalf of Americans but of an English monopoly. Resistance, boycott, and fighting became open between 1773 and 1775. The American war had begun. Nearly two-thirds of the tea then drunk in England was smuggled, and George III's Ministers did not scruple to share in the trade.

The American colonies were not one in this war, even after the Declaration of Independence in 1776. There were guerrillas fighting for England as bloodily as against her; and those who fought against England were not all Americans. George Washington won the American war when he did, mastering indifference, division, and treachery among his troops, in part at least because he could pay them with French loans and stiffen them with French troops and ships. The Americans who cornered an English army at Yorktown in 1781, and watched them march out to the tune of *The World Turned Upside Down*, had indeed won the war, against Ministers masterly and criminal in incompetence. But Benjamin Franklin had still to make the peace by which England acknowledged American Independence in 1783, in Paris: although, to make it, he consented to betray his French allies.

But it was not these causes, and not what the Americans had at stake, which stamped Blake's mind. What was urgent to Blake was what moved everyone in England in these years: the fight between principles which were believed to be at stake in England. Here, these principles were freed from the jealousies between the colonies, from the embarrassment of French and Spanish help, from American fanatics sacking the houses of exiles, and from profiteers buying them with paper money. In England what was at stake was thought of very simply. Bigoted Ministers were enforcing laws which were flatly against the wishes of England and America alike. And they were doing so by means which no Government should use against its own people. Therefore Edmund Burke, that overwound machine for saying uncommonly whatever was common talk, aimed his attacks at Government tyranny and bigotry.

> I am not one of those who think that the people are never in the wrong. They have been so, frequently and outrageously, both in other countries and in this. But I do say, that in all disputes between them and their rulers, the presumption is at least upon a par in favour of the people.

> The question with me is, not whether you have a right to render your people miserable; but whether it is not in your interest to make them happy. It is not, what a lawyer tells me, I *may* do; but what humanity, reason, and justice, tell me, I ought to do.

And the Black and Tan means used against the Americans aroused greater bitterness. The Ministers were shamefaced, but they could hardly do without Red Indians and German mercenaries. English dissenters and others felt kin only to the men who fought for America. Paid armies had never been liked in England; but hitherto, war had not been disliked. The great English patriotic songs had just become well known: Henry Fielding's and Richard Leveridge's two versions of *The Roast Beef of Old England*, about 1733; James Thomson's *Rule Britannia*, in 1740; *God Save the King*, in 1745; and David Garrick's *Heart of Oak*, in 1759. During the American war one broadside, *The British Grenadiers* of 1780, tried to rouse their fervour again. But a poem printed in 1782, *The Drum* of John Scott of Amwell, set down the mood which could find readers for the first time during the American war.

> I hate that drum's discordant sound,
> Parading round, and round, and round:
> To thoughtless youth it pleasure yields,
> And lures from cities and from fields,
> To sell their liberty for charms
> Of tawdry lace, and glittering arms;
> And when Ambition's voice commands,
> To march, and fight, and fall, in foreign lands.

> I hate that drum's discordant sound,
> Parading round, and round, and round:
> To me it talks of ravag'd plains,
> And burning towns, and ruin'd swains,
> And mangled limbs, and dying groans,
> And widows' tears, and orphans' moans;
> And all that Misery's hand bestows,
> To fill the catalogue of human woes.

John Scott was a Quaker, bold enough soberly to speak the Quaker mind. And his poem did not pass without attack. But the feeling against war for which he speaks moved all enlightened men, and moved them for the first time, during the American war. We may read the same feeling in the boyhood *Poetical Sketches*, which Blake printed in 1783—probably with the same printer who printed John Scott's poems. We may see it in two drawings which Blake showed at the Royal Academy in 1784, *War Unchained by an*

Angel—Fire, Pestilence, and Famine Following, and strikingly in
A Breach in the City—The Morning after a Battle. We may go on
reading it in the *Auguries of Innocence*, which Blake wrote later,
during the French wars.

> The Strongest Poison ever known
> Came from Caesar's Laurel Crown.
> Nought can deform the Human Race
> Like to the Armour's iron brace.   433

And Blake always held this feeling in the whole context made by
the American war and the England of his time: the context of
tyranny and poverty, as well as of war. As a boy, he had set the
scene for *Gwin, King of Norway* thus, in the *Poetical Sketches*.

> The Nobles of the land did feed
>   Upon the hungry Poor;
> They tear the poor man's lamb, and drive
>   The needy from their door!   11

As a man, he saw war in that larger context.

> The Beggar's Rags, fluttering in Air,
> Does to Rags the Heavens tear.
> The Soldier, arm'd with Sword & Gun,
> Palsied strikes the Summer's Sun.
> The poor Man's Farthing is worth more
> Than all the Gold on Afric's Shore.
> One Mite wrung from the Labrer's hands
> Shall buy & sell the Miser's Lands:
> Or, if protected from on high,
> Does that whole Nation sell & buy.   432

SEVEN

Two causes had thrust independence early on a fairly unwilling
America. Of course one, in England, was George III's wish to rule
England without her ruling interests. He could rule so only by
setting one faction against another, the City against the West
Indian Planters, the East India Company against the parliamentary
nabobs who had enriched themselves in the Company's service.
Divided in principle, and divided by such intrigues, England was
never likely to win with decision. But the larger cause was in America: that the colonies, scattered, jealous, and of many minds, were

against any single Government. Only because Ministers tried to force on them a strong single Government in England did they choose a weak single Government in America. The unwilling choice could still help to make civil war in 1861; and is not yet forgotten in American politics.

Yet the king who ruled by division, and who had lost thirteen colonies by overriding their divisions, found England moving together behind his Minister, within a year; and in half a dozen years knew her single-minded and of his own mind. Even before the end of 1783, Charles James Fox's bill to rule India under Whig patronage was petitioned against not only by the shaky East India Company, but by City merchants who might have welcomed this slackening of the Company's monopoly. George III felt strong enough to kill the Bill by his most outrageous message to the Lords, that 'he should deem those who should vote for the bill not only not his friends but his enemies'. Next year, England's pocketful of voters—three hundred thousand in a population of eight millions—entrenched the king's new tool, William Pitt the younger, then twenty-five, as Prime Minister for eighteen years. The City gave Pitt its freedom, and Wilkes stood for the Government. The Whig Opposition lost a hundred and sixty seats.

It was perhaps a first step in that moving together of nabobs and squires, planters and peers, merchants, manufacturers, and Tories, which became plain after the French Revolution. Perhaps the movement of fear was beginning: the causes of fear were coming over the horizon. In place of the smiling years before 1757, there were high prices, heavier taxes, and a growing, hungry population. There was a new anger in the crowd, and a harsh will to destroy. Riot had always been 'part of the mode of government' of a society whose poor had no vote and no Press. In 1769 Benjamin Franklin had seen

> within a year, riots in this country about corn; riots about elections; riots about workhouses; riots of colliers; riots of weavers; riots of coalheavers; riots of sawyers; riots of sailors, riots of Wilkites, riots of government chairmen, riots of smugglers.

But now the riots ceased to have heroes, and perhaps an understood aim. The six or seven good years which followed the American peace, and which made Pitt's name, put off the fear a little longer. But there had been a riot in 1780 which had put the fear of God even into those who had not been loth to see it begin.

Just who these were has never become plain. The sixty thousand men who marched from St George's Fields to Westminster on 2 June 1780 were petitioning for the repeal of a Roman Catholic Relief Act, which was then two years old. But on that day the Duke of Richmond was moving a Whig Suffrage Bill, which George III certainly disliked as much as he had disliked the Relief Act. On the other hand, the leader of the petition, Lord George Gordon, was seconded by Alderman Frederick Bull, a Member for the City of London and tool of Wilkes. The City had long been skilful in the raising of such riots, for example on behalf of Wilkes; and had not scrupled to give them a religious air, for example against the Jewish Naturalization Act in 1753. There is no doubt that the rioters took orders from Bull and other City men, at a linen draper's house in the Minories. For the City certainly wished to overthrow the Government, then at its weakest, and so to end the American war. It may have hoped to get rid of George III, who was known to be bracing himself to abdicate. But by an ironic chance, the timing of the riots may also have chimed happily with George III's own dislikes.

That night the rioters sacked the chapels of foreign embassies, among them one near Golden Square, where Blake lived over his father's hosier's shop. On the following nights their attacks spread from Roman Catholic houses to those of Ministers, magistrates, judges, and bishops; and then to courts, prisons, and public buildings. Franklin in Paris heard of the gutting of the house of the Chief Justice of the King's Bench with a pleasure which speaks all the bitterness of the American war,

> Among the rest Lord Mansfield's house is burnt with all his furniture, pictures, books and papers. Thus he who approved the burning of American houses, has had fire brought home to him.

On 6 June the rioters burned Newgate prison. On 7 June there were fires throughout the City, and the Bank of England was attacked. The rioters were going too far. That day, urged by the Opposition, George III issued a military proclamation. Troops were brought in to hold the three bridges and the main streets and buildings. Wilkes was now firing with the militia, and other City men grew warm in their duty. Though the rioters attacked the Bank again on 8 June, they were beaten off. London was fairly quiet by the following night; and other cities did as London did. About 300 rioters had been killed, and more wounded. Of 160 others tried, only sixty-two were condemned to death, and in fact only twenty-five were hanged: so plain was it that the leaders had not been taken. Most of those taken were hardly more than children.

In the upshot, the Gordon riots saved the falling Government. And they showed that the easy, riotous crowd of the eighteenth century could no longer be raised and handled at will. The talk of reform began to falter. Whigs drifted into Pitt's following, the Duke of Richmond among the first. Burke began to wonder whether still 'the presumption is at least upon a par in favour of the people'. And more stable men than Burke began to look askance at the round Declaration which had sounded noble in 1776.

> We hold these truths to be self-evident, that all men are created equal, that they are endowed by their Creator with certain unalienable Rights, that among these are Life, Liberty and the pursuit of Happiness – That to secure these rights, Governments are instituted among Men, deriving their just powers from the consent of the governed, – That whenever any Form of Government becomes destructive of these ends, it is the Right of the People to alter or to abolish it, and to institute new Government, laying its foundation on such principles, and organizing its powers in such form, as to them shall seem most likely to effect their Safety and Happiness. Prudence, indeed, will dictate that Governments long established should not be changed for light and transient causes; and accordingly all experience hath shown, that mankind are more disposed to suffer, while evils are sufferable, than to right themselves by abolishing the forms to which they are accustomed. But when a long train of abuses and usurpations, pursuing invariably the same Object, evinces a design to reduce them under absolute Despotism, it is their right, it is their duty, to throw off such Government, and to provide new Guards for their future security.

The Seditious Writings

ONE

William Blake was among those at the head of the crowd which burned Newgate prison on 6 June 1780: and his drawing which is usually called *Glad Day* may be meant to applaud the rising. He seems indeed to have been carried there by chance; and we know of others in the crowd who took no part in the burning, among them the poet George Crabbe. Crabbe had then just come to London to the patronage of Burke, of which Blake wrote with contempt later in the bitter years of the French wars. Unlike Burke, Crabbe kept his sympathy with the poor; and Blake did not grow afraid of the crowd, then or later. Both poets, young men in their twenties, began to look away from the eighteenth-century manner, into a world seen solidly by its shadows. This is the movement of Crabbe's mind from *The Library* to *The Village*.

> No; cast by Fortune on a frowning coast,
> Which neither groves nor happy valleys boast;
> Where other cares than those the Muse relates,
> And other Shepherds dwell with other mates;
> By such examples taught, I paint the Cot,
> As truth will paint it and as bards will not.
> Nor you, ye Poor, of letter'd scorn complain,
> To you the smoothest song is smooth in vain;
> O'ercome by labour and bow'd down by time,
> Feel you the barren flattery of a rhyme?
> Can Poets sooth you, when you pine for bread,
> By winding myrtles round your ruin'd shed?

nd this is the movement of Blake from the *Poetical Sketches* to
he like wish of the *Songs of Innocence,* to find a symbolism more
obust than the eighteenth-century picnic.

Blake was a man whose mind moved slowly; and between 1780
nd 1790 he had to find his place in the bodily world as well as in
hat of the mind. His apprenticeship had ended in 1779, and he had
narried in 1782. He was earning his living by working hard at hack-
work. After his father's death in 1784 Blake opened a print-shop
vith a fellow engraver, and took his brother Robert with him. The
hop seems not to have done well, and was given up after Robert's
leath three years later. Meanwhile, Blake was reading Swedenborg
nd other odd, self-willed men. He drifted into and out of the
riendship of pious liberals of vague goodwill, such as the Reverend
Anthony Stephen Mathew and his blue-stocking wife. Blake had
written nothing now for ten years. But his mind was becoming his
own; and about 1784 he began a satire which set him to writing the
Songs of Innocence.

This satire, which is commonly called *An Island in the Moon,* is
imed in the main at the utilitarians and cranks whom Blake had
met at the Mathews'. But there are others in it who belong to less
ationalist sets. Steelyard the Lawgiver, whose name caricatures the
cales of Justice (a steelyard is a Roman balance), is a Whig of the
patriotic age.

> 'Hm,' said the Lawgiver, 'Funny enough! Let's have handel's
> water piece.' Then Sipsop sung:
>> 'A crowned king,
>> On a white horse sitting,
>> With his trumpets sounding,
>> And Banners flying,
> Thro' the clouds of smoke he makes his way,
> And the shout of his thousands fills his heart with rejoicing &
>> victory:
> And the shout of his thousands fills his heart with rejoicing &
>> victory.
> Victory! Victory! 'twas William, the prince of Orange,—' 62

For Handel had been Court composer in the great Whig reign of
George II. Pope had sneered magnificently at George II's reluctance
to go to war and his philistinism together,

> While You, great Patron of Mankind, sustain
> The balanc'd World, and open all the Main;
> Your Country, chief, in Arms abroad defend,
> At home, with Morals, Arts, and Laws amend;
> How shall the Muse, from such a Monarch, steal
> An hour, and not defraud the Publick Weal?

Nevertheless, in George II's reign the Whigs, who had once brought William III from Orange, had won an empire for England. The towns had grown evil in his reign. But also, men had come to take white bread and leather shoes for granted, and had learnt to speak of comfort: they had made the cry 'Roast Beef' English for 'Eureka'. To Blake's mind now, George III's American war had made the patriotic songs of that age false also. *An Island in the Moon* recalls Leveridge's lines,

> Our Fathers of old were robust, stout, and strong,
> And kept open House with good Cheer all Day long,
> Which made their plump Tenants rejoice in this song,
> > *Oh the Roast Beef of* Old England,
> > *And* Old English *Roast Beef.*

But it recalls them as model for a satire sung by Steelyard the Lawgiver.

> This city & this country has brought forth many mayors,
> To sit in state & give forth laws out of their old oak chairs,
> With face as brown as any nut with drinking of strong ale;
> Good English hospitality, O then it did not fail!
>
> > With scarlet gowns & broad gold lace would make a yeoman
> > sweat,
> With stockings roll'd above their knees & shoes as black as jet,
> With eating beef & drinking beer, O they were stout & hale!
> Good English hospitality, O then it did not fail!
>
> > Thus sitting at the table wide, the Mayor & Aldermen
> Were fit to give law to the city; each eat as much as ten.
> The hungry poor enter'd the hall, to eat good beef & ale.
> Good English hospitality, O then it did not fail!   58

The poor in the Gordon riots also had begun by cheering the Lord Mayor, and ended by attacking the Mansion House. And often since Blake's birth, the hungry poor had been rioting for bread in and out of London. Steelyard the Lawgiver leaves no doubt that the Island in the Moon was larger than Mrs Mathew's drawing-room; and leaves no doubt where in that island Blake's sympathy fell.

TWO

About the time that Blake was writing *An Island in the Moon*, he had begun to meet more radical men at the house of the bookseller Joseph Johnson. Although *An Island in the Moon* mocks their owlish and long-winded foibles, it shows also on what grounds Blake met them. One such ground was the hatred of war which the American war had prompted. And the American war had enlarged a common hatred of all the tools for forcing unwelcome government on men who had chosen their own. These remained the grounds on which, half a dozen years later, the war against the French Revolution was attacked by the more liberal Whigs: Fox, Grey, Sheridan, Erskine, Whitbread, the Dukes of Bedford and of Norfolk. But Blake shared with Joseph Johnson's radicals a more searching hatred for the subtler tools of oppression: poverty, ignorance, and government itself. Steelyard the Lawgiver is already that false 'Albion the punisher & judge' whom Blake saw to the end of his life as one who

> sat by Tyburn's brook, and underneath his heel shot up
> A deadly Tree: he nam'd it Moral Virtue and the Law
> Of God.   65²

Blake was already of the mind which he set down plainly at the beginning of the war against the French Revolution,

> In the North, to Odin, Sotha gave a Code of War,
> Because of Diralada, thinking to reclaim his joy.
> These were the Churches, Hospitals, Castles, Palaces,
> Like nets & gins & traps to catch the joys of Eternity,
>   And all the rest a desart;
> Till, like a dream, Eternity was obliterated & erased.
>
> Thus the terrible race of Los & Enitharmon gave
> Laws & Religions to the sons of Har, binding them more

F

And more to Earth, closing and restraining,
Till a Philosophy of Five Senses was complete.
Urizen wept & gave it into the hands of Newton & Locke. 246

Here and elsewhere, when Blake thinks of his society he attacks its religion. Now that the last commandments are less well remembered than by-laws, we tend to yawn through these attacks. But the religious changes of Blake's lifetime were urgent to him and to his fellows. The rationalism which had grown in the Church during the Whig age was being formalized, for example by William Paley, who saw God as a strict designer for use. But even this 'Philosophy of Five Senses' was no longer rigid enough for the Church. Paley got no preferment, and George III thought him 'a dangerous revolutionary'. At the same time the revival which John Wesley had been leading since 1739 was breaking the old link between dissent and political freedom. Wesley alone among dissenters had upheld George III in the American war. The men who met at Joseph Johnson's were not of one religious mind. There was among them a Roman Catholic Bible critic; and Johnson printed the evangelical poems of Cowper. Nevertheless, these men were the last defenders of the liberal tradition of dissent. Many of them were Unitarians from the great dissenting academies, tolerant even of other Unitarians. Of the two outstanding Unitarians who met at Johnson's, Joseph Priestley looked for the bases of religion rationally, in experience. But Richard Price did not wholly share this deism: and held that man has an inborn knowledge of right and wrong, in innocence.

Blake had gone neither to the dissenting academies nor to any other school. His father had been a dissenter who may have known of Swedenborg. Blake's friends Flaxman and Butts belonged to the following of Swedenborg, and Blake leaned to it. Yet, unlike Swedenborg's, Blake's robust mysticism did not underrate experience. Rather Blake shared the belief of Price, that the content of experience is not merely rational. He believed that experience comes to man from outside, but is shaped in him always as human experience. It was this feeling of humanity which made him value Lavater's glib *Aphorisms on Man*. We may read it in the first two aphorisms,

Know, in the first place, that mankind agree in essence, as they do in their limbs and senses.

> Mankind differ as much in essence as they do in form, limbs, and senses—and only so, and not more,

beside which Blake wrote,

> This is true Christian philosophy far above all abstraction.   65

Henry Fuseli had just translated these *Aphorisms*, and Joseph Johnson had printed them in 1788 with a plate engraved by Blake after Fuseli. In reading Lavater and Swedenborg together, Blake was trying to work out a common form for dissent. He was trying to fit experience to innocence. It is the theme of all that he wrote in these years.

This is the starting point, in 1789, of the prophetic books *Tiriel* and *The Book of Thel*, as plainly as of the *Songs of Innocence*. Both prophetic books set out the same belief, that knowledge is not bounded by the senses, but that it must be made actual through the senses. The virgin Thel, who has held back from experience, finds knowledge only in death. Blake is using the symbol of death as the eighteenth century had once used the word, to mean the experience of sex. The old man Tiriel, the blind hypocrite of will, thinks it wisdom to enslave the sons who are his rebellious thoughts, and the five daughters who are his senses; but he and they suffer the horrors of *King Lear* until he learns to free them from such wisdom and its laws. Both books ask the same question in the same words,

> Can Wisdom be put in a silver rod?
> Or Love in a golden bowl?   127

And both answer that experience is neither gold nor silver, but earthen.

Blake took this questioning farthest in *The Marriage of Heaven and Hell*. The simple proverbs and visions of this book are still religious parables. And they begin from religious thoughts: from Swedenborg's *Vision of Heaven and Hell*, and from two notes which Blake wrote in the margin of Swedenborg's *Wisdom of Angels Concerning Divine Love and Divine Wisdom*,

> Good & Evil are here both Good & the two contraries Married.   91
> Heaven & Hell are born together.   96

But now the force which holds experience to innocence is no longer mystic. The reasoning begins as in *Tiriel* and *The Book of Thel*. What is known is good only so long as it is experienced. When knowledge forgets the experience in which it lived, it becomes the contradiction of experience, rigid and evil:

> Prisons are built with stones of Law, Brothels with bricks of Religion. 151

Therefore only that which knowledge calls evil is then experienced and truly good. Experience must now be charged, explosively, with innocence:

> The tygers of wrath are wiser than the horses of instruction. 152

This energy, which makes a single urge and judgement of innocence within experience, is the new force of *The Marriage of Heaven and Hell*. From this time, energy becomes the core of Blake's religious thought. There is here a striking hint of the crime story, in which the anti-social crowd of the eighteenth century was happy: evil and energy exploding society for its good. This anarchism remains masterful in Blake's prophetic books.

THREE

The time-table of the prophetic books is fairly certainly known. Blake wrote *Tiriel* about 1789, and etched *The Book of Thel* in the same year. *The Marriage of Heaven and Hell* was etched between 1790 and 1793; and all copies of it have for last pages *A Song of Liberty*, although this may not have been written as part of it. In 1793 Blake etched *Visions of the Daughters of Albion* and *America*, and in 1794 *Europe* and *The Book of Urizen*. In 1795 he etched *The Book of Ahania*, *The Book of Los*, and *The Song of Los*. He wrote *Vala or The Four Zoas* at times between 1795 and 1804, leaving it in a manuscript which he had dated 1797. He etched *Milton* and *Jerusalem* after 1804.

These dates are not chance: they are the forgotten key to much that is secret in the manner of the prophetic books. The manner is of a piece with the vague grandiloquence of their names, *Tiriel*, *The Book of Ahania*, *Vala or The Four Zoas*. But the list shows a set of names which bear recognizably on the world which we know: *A Song of Liberty*, *Visions of the Daughters of Albion*, *America*, and *Europe*. All these were written between 1790 and 1794, and probably towards the end of this time. In *Tiriel*, in *The Book of Thel*, and in *The Marriage of Heaven and Hell*, Blake had moved from the attack on the religion of 'Thou shalt not' step by step to the attack on law. Now, in the books written between 1790 and 1794, he turned this attack on law frankly upon the England of his time. And he left no doubt of his social aim when, in 1790 or 1791, he began a book which he simply called *The French Revolution*.

In order that we may be sure that the Albion, the America, and the Europe of these books are the places which we know by these names, let us look at them in the first lines of *A Song of Liberty*.

1. The Eternal Female groan'd! it was heard over all the Earth.

2. Albion's coast is sick, silent; the American meadows faint!

3. Shadows of Prophecy shiver along by the lakes and the rivers, and mutter across the ocean: France, rend down thy dungeon!

4. Golden Spain, burst the barriers of old Rome!

5. Cast thy keys, O Rome, into the deep down falling, even to eternity down falling.

6. And weep.

7. In her trembling hands she took the new born terror, howling.

8. On those infinite mountains of light, now barr'd out by the atlantic sea, the new born fire stood before the starry king!

9. Flag'd with grey brow'd snows and thunderous visages, the jealous wings wav'd over the deep.

10. The speary hand burned aloft, unbuckled was the shield; forth went the hand of jealousy among the flaming hair, and hurl'd the new born wonder thro' the starry night.

11. The fire, the fire is falling!

12. Look up! look up! O citizen of London, enlarge thy countenance! O Jew, leave counting gold! return to thy oil and wine. O African! black African! (go, winged thought, widen his forehead.) 159

This is not a fable about the Eternal Female and the 'infinite mountains of light' of Atlantis. It is a piece of rhetoric about the French Revolution, seen as the first outcome of the American revolt; and it calls for a like outcome the world over. Nor is it tactfully guarded in its calls. The call to the Roman Catholic Church might be forgiven, in the biblical setting of the verses. But the call to Spain raised an echo which went on troubling English Ministers for twenty-five years, perhaps for a hundred and fifty years.

> It was in Spain that the British policy was most completely stultified. Ferdinand VII restored the Inquisition, abolished the Constitution, and imprisoned or executed the leading Liberals, the very men who admired most fervently the fundamental principles of English political and social life. To re-establish his despotism the Spanish King employed troops paid with British gold and led by British officers. The Opposition at Westminster raised violent protests, and the Ministry scarcely dared to defend their action. The Cabinet even admitted that were any intervention in Spain admissible, it would be against absolutism. They were well aware—their ambassador at Madrid had informed them of it—that every success of absolutism in the Peninsula was so much loss to British influence.

So wrote Halévy, in 1912; he was writing of the year 1814. Long before that year, the Sedition Acts had silenced every call to the 'citizen of London'. But even the call to the black African was not wise. For about the time that Blake wrote A Song of Liberty, the movement to end slavery suffered two set-backs: the slaves of French Haiti revolted; and the French Convention, without irony, made William Wilberforce a French citizen. The Jew alone was left no choice but to do as Blake asked; for the Bank of England stopped paying gold in 1797.

FOUR

A Song of Liberty is rhetorical, and therefore is vague. But those to whom it calls are actual, and what it says to them is apt. So The French Revolution, Visions of the Daughters of Albion, America, and Europe are named and written to catch other eyes than those which might linger on Tiriel and The Book of Thel. In the years 1790 to 1794 Blake felt that what he had to say should reach as many men as it could. He had printed no book since Flaxman and Mrs Mathew had printed his boyhood Poetical Sketches in 1783.

He had left *Tiriel* in manuscript, and etched *The Book of Thel* himself. He did one or the other with everything else that he wrote, except once. When he began *The French Revolution*, in 1790 or 1791, he did not etch it: he set about having it printed. And he wrote it more directly, in its orator's manner, than anything else which he wrote.

Yet *The French Revolution* was not printed; it was not even finished. And in the other books of these very years the writing from page to page grows vaguer and thicker. The rhetoric clogs and mumbles with unheard names, Oothoon, Orc, Enitharmon; and we are suddenly aware that Blake has wandered off into those mazes of their family troubles which henceforth fill his prophetic books. This is not mysticism, but mystery, and mystification. Why should Blake choose to play at it at the one time when he felt it urgent to speak to more than the fifty friends who bought his poems? How did he come to turn back from this urgency so soon, how did he come to turn at all, to the roaring but dumb harangues of the prophetic books?

These puzzles reach back to a simpler question: Why was *The French Revolution* not printed? It was to have been printed in seven books, perhaps without Blake's name, for Joseph Johnson. We have a proof copy of the first book, dated 1791, and giving its price as a shilling: so that we know that this book was set. It may be that Joseph Johnson then came to doubt whether the book would sell. But he had little to lose by printing and binding so cheap a book, once it had been set. Certainly, if Johnson doubted whether the book would sell, it was not because he had changed his mind about the French Revolution; but because others had. The mind of England was visibly clouding and lowering. After Louis XVI had tried to fly from France in June 1791, English newspapers began to print rumours that there would be rioting if the fall of the Bastille were again toasted in England in July. Punctually a well-schooled crowd in Birmingham sacked the houses of Joseph Priestley and of other dissenters. Joseph Johnson still went on to print Mary Wollstonecraft's *Vindication of the Rights of Woman* in 1792, and William Godwin's *Enquiry Concerning Political Justice* in 1793. The Government had let it be known that it did not trouble itself about such highly priced books. But Johnson had been wary of another cheap book: and this, precisely in 1791. Early in that year he had been printing the first part of Tom Paine's *Rights of Man*; and, suddenly and sensationally, had turned it over to another printer, after some copies had already been printed with his own name. This was a book of whose sales Johnson had no doubt. He gave it up because, in 1791, he saw the attack on the Press blowing up. It blew up in May 1792, in the Royal Proclamation against Divers Wicked Seditious Writings; and Paine and his printer were prose-cuted after the second part of *The Rights of Man*. In September 1792 another warrant was issued against Paine for a speech which he had just made to the Friends of the People. It was Blake who packed him off from Joseph Johnson's to France (so the story goes), twenty minutes before the warrant followed him to Dover.

There had been many signs of the political bad weather to come, between 1789 and 1791; and men less shrewd than Joseph Johnson had read them. But no one could guess how fierce the storm to come would be. At the time of the Proclamation against Seditious Writings there had been little violence in France. There had been nothing in England more threatening than the founding of the London Corresponding Society, a penny-a-week club of working-men for parliamentary reform; and of the Friends of the People, a Whig club with the same aim at two and a half guineas a year. Meanwhile, the European kings had founded their own alliance; and the Duke of Brunswick, marching on France, proclaimed their policy as slaughter of all who threatened Louis XVI. Only after this proclamation, in August 1792, did the Paris crowd storm the Tuileries, and begin the first Terror of September. The crowd could hardly guess that the Austrian Minister was then writing,

> The re-establishment of order is no longer to be considered the most important object of our military operations. The continuance of disorder and civil war must even be regarded as favourable to our cause, and the return of peace, consequent on the arrangement of a French Constitution of some kind, will be a benefit which France will have to purchase by the sacrifice of the province we shall have conquered.

Nevertheless, the crowd drove the Duke of Brunswick's army into Holland, and began the trial of Louis XVI. In England, the younger Pitt grew hysterical at Cabinet meetings—'Probably by this time to-morrow we may not have a hand to act, or a tongue to utter'—and called up part of the militia, on the ground of acts of riot and insurrection. Where were these acts? asked Fox. The answer was folded away in a letter which the mainstay of Pitt's Government, Lord Grenville, had just written to a loyal alarmist.

> It is not unnatural, nor is it an unfavourable symptom, that people who are thoroughly frightened, as the body of landed gentlemen in this country are, should exaggerate these stories as they pass from one mouth to the other; but you who know the course of this sort of reports, ought not too hastily to give credit to them.

In January 1793 Louis XVI was found guilty, and was beheaded. On 1 February England went to war with France, on a Dutch issue: for Holland had a treaty claim on England. Holland, if she made her claim, did not choose to make it public.

In 1793 men calling for parliamentary reform in Scotland were savagely sentenced by Lord Justice Clerk Braxfield, whom even the Government thought a 'violent and intemperate great man' in private. In 1794 the leaders of the London Corresponding Society were charged with treason, while Parliament suspended Habeas Corpus in one sitting. Thomas Erskine broke the charge by breaking the evidence of the spies whom the Government had put into the Society. It was now plain how Pitt came by his fears: for spies have to make their stories seem worth the buying. Even Pitt's friend Wilberforce found 'his sanguine temper leading him to give credit to information which others might distrust'. His biographer Charles Whibley is more lyrical.

> This sternly practical sense persuaded him also to reject no instrument that might prove useful to him. No Minister has ever employed spies on so vast a scale or to so good a purpose. The man who brought him valuable information never went empty away. He had learned from his father the power of knowledge, and he had improved upon the lesson.

The year 1795 was a year of great dearth. There were huge bread riots; and George III, on his way to Parliament, was mobbed by a crowd shouting for peace. The Government answered with Bills, against Seditious Meetings, and against Treasonable Practices,

which included anything which might 'excite or stir up to hatred
or contempt of the person of his Majesty'. It is hardly worth
taking the endless list farther: to the Newspaper Act of 1798, to
the Act of 1799 against Seditious Societies, and to the Combination Laws of the same year. For in 1796 the French armies had
become the armies of Napoleon Bonaparte. The French Revolution had been defeated, by intervention from without, and by the
moneyed middlemen within, whom Mary Wollstonecraft had seen
and feared in Paris in 1793:

> If the aristocracy of birth is levelled with the ground, only to
> make room for that of riches, I am afraid that the morals of
> the people will not be much improved by the change, or the
> government rendered less venal.

The second Terror, from the summer of 1793 to that of 1794, had
done its work, within and without. England was not reminded
that, throughout the French wars, there were probably fewer men
executed in France than were hanged by law in England. Meanwhile the Attorney General, Lord Eldon to be, had noted in 1795
of the Sedition Acts,

> that in the last two years there had been more prosecutions for
> libels than in any twenty years before.

FIVE

Could *The French Revolution* of Blake have been called a seditious libel? The first book tells the story of the revolution simply,
but does not take it far. It does not even reach the fall of the
Bastille. It is written plainly and with open sympathy, and it
might have been widely read. Of course, *The French Revolution*,
being meant for printing, is not as outspoken as are some verses
which Blake wrote privately in his commonplace book about the
same time.

> 'Let the Brothels of Paris be opened
> 'With many an alluring dance,
> 'To awake the Physicians thro' the city,'
> Said the beautiful Queen of France.

> The King awoke on his couch of gold,
> As soon as he heard these tidings told:
> 'Arise & come, both fife & drum,
> 'And the [Famine] shall eat both crust & crumb.'
>   [Then he swore a great & solemn Oath:
> 'To kill the people I am loth,
> 'But If they rebel, they must go to hell:
> 'They shall have a Priest & a passing bell.']   185

But in meaning and implication, *The French Revolution* does not differ from this. It would certainly have been thought wrong-headed by the frightened gentlemen of 1791; and it might have been thought dangerous. We cannot even be sure that, because the proof copy is dated 1791, it was ready to be printed before the Proclamation against Seditious Writings was made, on 21 May 1792. There are sentences which Blake put into the mouths of Louis XVI's evil counsellors which would have sounded awkwardly when Louis XVI was taking just such advice, and when the Duke of Brunswick was marshalling his army.

> Thy Nobles have gather'd thy starry hosts round this rebellious city,
> To rouze up the ancient forests of Europe, with clarions of cloud breathing war,
> To hear the horse neigh to the drum and trumpet, and the trumpet and war shout reply.
> Stretch the hand that beckons the eagles of heaven; they cry over Paris, and wait
> Till Fayette point his finger to Versailles; the eagles of heaven must have their prey!   138

And England would no longer have welcomed the advice of the good counsellor, that a free people makes a free and secure government.

> Is the body diseas'd when the members are healthful? can the man be bound in sorrow
> Whose ev'ry function is fill'd with its fiery desire? can the soul whose brain and heart
> Cast their rivers in equal tides thro' the great Paradise, languish because the feet,

Hands, head, bosom, and parts of love follow their high
breathing joy?
And can Nobles be bound when the people are free, or God
weep when his children are happy?
Have you never seen Fayette's forehead, or Mirabeau's eyes,
or the shoulders of Target,
Or Bailly the strong foot of France, or Clermont the terrible
voice? and your robes
Still retain their own crimson: mine never yet faded, for fire
delights in its form.
But go, merciless man! enter into the infinite labyrinth of
another's brain
Ere thou measure the circle that he shall run. Go, thou cold
recluse, into the fires
Of another's high flaming rich bosom, and return unconsum'd,
and write laws.
If thou canst not do this, doubt thy theories; learn to consider
all men as thy equals,
Thy brethren, and not as thy foot or thy hand, unless thou first
fearest to hurt them.   142

Blake is here writing out fully the dislike of Locke's narrow ideal
of equality before the law, which he had put into *Tiriel* and *The
Marriage of Heaven and Hell*: 'One Law for the Lion & Ox is
Oppression'. He is writing it in the very language of the two
aphorisms of Lavater which were to him 'true Christian philosophy far above all abstraction'. Blake held to this philosophy of
fulfilment all his life. He wrote in *Jerusalem*,

In Great Eternity every particular Form gives forth or Ema-
nates
Its own peculiar Light, & the Form is the Divine Vision
And the Light is his Garment. This is Jerusalem in every Man,
A Tent & Tabernacle of Mutual Forgiveness, Male & Female
Clothings.
And Jerusalem is called Liberty among the Children of Albion.
But Albion fell down.   684

And the philosophy has itself grown fuller. It has taken on an
imagery apt to its time, of which *The Marriage of Heaven and
Hell* gave glimpses: 'Bring out number, weight & measure in a
year of dearth'. But, precisely because of its social aptness, this

Christian philosophy was no longer welcome as a philosophy of law. It is not out of place to read here a letter which a just judge, Lord Ellenborough, wrote to Wilberforce in 1802, about slavery.

> I have always felt a great abhorrence of the mode by which these unfortunate creatures are torn from their families and country, and have doubted whether any sound policy could grow out of a system which seemed to be so vicious in its foundation; but I am extremely alarmed at the consequence of disturbing it, particularly in the present convulsed state of the world. In short, my dear sir, I am almost ashamed to say that I tremble at giving their full effect to the impressions which the subject naturally makes on my mind, in the first view of it, as a man and a Christian. I am frightened at the consequences of any innovation upon a long-established practice, at a period so full of dangers as the present. At the same time I cannot well reconcile it with the will of God.

In such times a less scrupulous lawyer had little trouble in reading sedition in Christian philosophy. At a pinch, Lord Eldon could no doubt tell a jury just how, in the republic, the 'parts of love follow their high breathing joy'.

The French Revolution was given up between setting and printing, because what it said had grown to be disliked in that time; and it may have grown to be thought seditious. Its suppression turned Blake back to the private manner which *The French Revolution* had been leaving. For *The French Revolution* was written to be read, and to be understood, by simple men. It was happy to have for symbols of its spiritual struggle the happenings of a real world. It is no less symbolical than the other prophetic books, earlier and later. But its manner is vivid and direct: round as the best of the later books, but simpler.

> But the dens shook and trembled: the prisoners look up and
>   assay to shout; they listen,
> Then laugh in the dismal den, then are silent, and a light
>   walks around the dark towers.   136

Swinburne was not unjust when he called this 'mere wind and splutter': although the judgement comes with odd authority from him. For it is what Blake called *Jerusalem*, speech 'in the mouth

of a true Orator' rather than of a poet. But it is moving an
understandable speech; and although Blake's later speech is bett
as it grows more assured, it is not better for being vaguer, and
is not better for being aimless. Unlike the later books, *The Frenc
Revolution* seldom lingers in the rhetoric for the sake of th
rhetoric. It is never loth to go on, as later books are, because the
is really nothing very different to go to. It never wanders from th
point, and it has a point. It has what Blake came most to lack,
forward aim and movement.

The French Revolution lets us see how Blake's manner migh
have grown, had Joseph Johnson printed the book a year earlie
and had it found the readers whom it might then have found. Tha
it was not printed made it an unhappy turning point in Blake'
writing. For when Blake went on to etch *Visions of the Daughter
of Albion* and *America*, in 1793, England was already at war witl
France, and the Terror was silencing all talk of the Revolution
Paine had gone to France, and Priestley was making ready to g
to America, stripped of the hopes which had meant more to hin
than his researches:

> As the world advances in civilization, and national animosity
> abates, war becomes less distressing to peaceable individuals
> who do not bear arms.

The wars of mercenaries were giving place to total war, and the
peaceable individuals were being pressed into the militia. The
Sedition Acts began to stand large over the written word. The pa
tient reader of *Visions of the Daughters of Albion* and *America*
can still trace Blake's hopes, symbolized in the sexual fulfilment of
these woman nations. And the lesson is still plain.

> Why trembles honesty, and like a murderer
> Why seeks he refuge from the frowns of his immortal station?
> Must the generous tremble & leave his joy to the idle, to the
>   pestilence,
> That mock him? who commanded this? what God? what
>   Angel?
> To keep the gen'rous from experience till the ungenerous
> Are unrestrain'd performers of the energies of nature;
> Till pity is become a trade, and generosity a science
> That men get rich by; & the sandy desert is giv'n to the strong?

What God is he writes laws of peace & clothes him in a
    tempest?
What pitying Angel lusts for tears and fans himself with sighs?
What crawling villain preaches abstinence & wraps himself
In fat of lambs? no more I follow, no more obedience pay! 200

But Blake has already thought it well to use the symbolism of
The Book of Thel in place of that of *The French Revolution*.
And he has thought it well to speak his hopes not of the French
Revolution but of the American revolt, which the Whigs had
made respectable.

Enslav'd, the Daughters of Albion weep; a trembling lamenta-
    tion
Upon their mountains; in their valleys, sighs toward America. 189

Yet Blake is certainly thinking of France. Having already quoted
the climax of *A Song of Liberty*, 'Empire is no more! and now the
Lion & Wolf shall cease', he ends *America* in the very words of
that song.

While he was etching *America*, Blake cancelled a plate in which
he had written of George III by name. Another year, and even
the names which run through *America*, Washing'.on, Franklin,
and Paine, must be hidden in less revolutionary symbols of energy,
Los and Orc. The horror of *Europe*, etched in 1794, is the horror
of the war against the French Revolution. But it has taken on
the smoky vagueness with which Blake was now clouding his
thought. Put beside the conflicts of *The French Revolution* those
of *Europe*,

Thus was the howl thro' Europe!
For Orc rejoic'd to hear the howling shadows;
But Palamabron shot his lightnings, trenching down his wide
    back;
And Rintrah hung with all his legions in the nether deep: 242

the change is deliberate, a disguise. Blake is here calling the forces
of the French Revolution Orc, and the forces against the Revolution Rintrah and Palamabron the 'horned priest', who 'tell the
Human race that Woman's love is Sin'. Blake chose to give these

forces such forms, because his mind worked in large and shifting abstractions. But he chose now to call these forms Orc, Rintrah, and Palamabron, because he dared not call them Lafayette, Pitt, and George III. Yet these are the men within these symbols. For example, although the meaning of the symbols came to change, Rintrah with the Plow in *Milton* remains the Plowman whom *The Spiritual Form of Pitt, Guiding Behemoth* orders 'to Plow up the Cities and Towers'. It is not easy to see that Blake is taking the French side in the war when he writes,

> But terrible Orc, when he beheld the morning in the east,
> Shot from the heights of Enitharmon,
> And in the vineyards of red France appear'd the light of his
>   fury.
>   The sun glow'd fiery red!
> The furious terrors flew around
> On golden chariots raging with red wheels dropping with
>   blood!
> The Lions lash their wrathful tails!
> The Tigers couch upon the prey & suck the ruddy tide,
> And Enitharmon groans & cries in anguish and dismay.   245

Nevertheless, he is taking the French side: and he would have been foolhardy to condone the Terror more openly than this. When Blake etched *Europe*, the leaders of the London Corresponding Society were awaiting trial. The shadows of the censor and the spy lay across the page; and Blake knew it. The most outspoken lines of *Europe* fix the shadow of 1794.

> Every house a den, every man bound: the shadows are fill'd
> With spectres, and the windows wove over with curses of iron:
> Over the doors 'Thou shalt not', & over the chimneys 'Fear'
>   is written:
> With bands of iron round their necks fasten'd into the walls
> The citizens, in leaden gyves the inhabitants of suburbs
> Walk heavy; soft and bent are the bones of villagers.   243

SIX

At the beginning of the war against the French Revolution, Blake put into his notebook a *Memorandum* which has puzzled his readers.

> I say I shan't live five years, And if I live one it will be a
> Wonder   June 1793   187

We do, however, know why, just five years later, Blake wrote on
the back of the title-page of a religious book,

> To defend the Bible in this year 1798 would cost a man his
> life.   383

These words have a long history. In 1789 Richard Price had
spoken before a dinner to toast the Glorious Whig Revolution of
1688; and had pointed the likeness to the French Revolution. In
1790 Edmund Burke attacked this speech in his *Reflections on
the Revolution in France*, and broke with the Whigs; he later sent
his son to France to rally those fighting against the Revolution.
Tom Paine had answered Burke in *The Rights of Man*, and had
got the hearing which he had sought since the American war. He
used it to broadcast the rationalism which Blake had heard him
argue at Joseph Johnson's. Between 1793 and 1795, Paine printed
the two parts of *The Age of Reason*, which argues not for atheism
but for deism. The Government prosecuted his printers; and it
prosecuted more than a hundred sellers of the book, for more than
thirty years. But it also wanted to have Paine answered; and it
wanted to have him answered as Price had been answered, not
by a Tory but by a Whig. This is how Richard Watson came to
write his *Apology for the Bible* in 1796, and how Blake came to
read the book. By way of thanks, George III said that he 'did not
know the Bible needed an apology'.

Richard Watson, like Paine, was now nearly sixty. He was of
the stamp of the ample, happy, broad-minded pluralists who had
flourished in the Whig age; but abler, more energetic, and less
scrupulous. He had been in turn professor of chemistry and of
divinity in the University of Cambridge. In order to qualify for
the latter chair, he had been given an honorary doctorate of
divinity, one day before the examination. The chair of chemistry
had not needed even so formal a qualification. The dignity with
which he wrote himself, on the title-page on which Blake was
writing, R. *Watson*, D.D., F.R.S., was therefore not the dignity
of labour. This, however, should be said for Watson's energy, that
he did think it his duty to learn something both of chemistry and
of divinity, when he was professor of them. His kindly Whig

divinity had earned him the names of the Levelling Prelate and the Bishop of the Dissenters. In 1780 he was writing with heat on behalf of the Whigs, against the Archbishop of York's charge that they had led the Gordon riots. In 1782, when the Whigs held the Government, he took a bishopric. He notes that it was agreed that he should write pamphlets for the Government from time to time, if they should be needed. Even so, he could get only the miserable Bishopric of Llandaff. In 1792 he wrote a pamphlet to recant his liberal past, and to grieve at the French Revolution as Burke had done. William Wordsworth had already attacked this pamphlet in 1793.

The notes which Blake now wrote on Watson's *Apology for the Bible* speak the anger of the revolutionary against the renegade.

> I have not the Charity for the Bishop that he pretends to have
> for Paine. I believe him to be a State trickster. Dishonest Mis-
> representation. Priestly Impudence. Contemptible Falsehood
> & Detraction. Presumptuous Murderer.   384
> The Beast & the Whore rule without control.   383

The Beast is the State, and the Whore is its Church. Blake took it for granted that Watson was writing for the Government and, whatever his title, was writing to uphold the war against the French Revolution.

> To what does the Bishop attribute the English Crusade against
> France? Is it not to State Religion? Blush for shame.   385

Against this conspiracy of State and 'the Abomination that maketh desolate, *i.e.* State Religion', Blake chose to uphold the deism of Paine, which he did not share. His choice was steadfast.

> The Perversions of Christ's words & acts are attack'd by Paine
> & also the perversions of the Bible.   383
> Paine has not attacked Christianity. Watson has defended
> Antichrist.   383
> It appears to me Now that Tom Paine is a better Christian
> than the Bishop.   396

Unlike Lord Ellenborough, Blake did not fear to be 'a man and a Christian'; and therefore stood with Paine, with revolt, with the energy of Milton's Satan, and with Hell as the fire of energy.

Blake's testament of faith, where Watson asks 'whether you have examined calmly', is eloquent.

> Paine is either a Devil or an Inspired man. Men who give themselves to their Energetic Genius in the manner that Paine does are no Examiners. If they are not determinately wrong they must be Right or the Bible is false; as to Examiners in these points they will be spewed out. The Man who pretends to be a modest enquirer into the truth of a self evident thing is a Knave. The truth & certainty of Virtue and Honesty, *i.e.* Inspiration, needs no one to prove it; it is Evident as the Sun & Moon. He who stands doubting of what he intends, whether it is Virtuous or Vicious, knows not what Virtue means. No man can do a Vicious action & think it to be Virtuous. No man can take darkness for light. He may pretend to do so & may pretend to be a modest Enquirer, but he is a Knave.   386

Feeling so strongly, and seeing the sides so sharply, why did Blake not take his notes beyond the margin of the book, and print them where they could be seen? Blake has given us the answer himself, in a set of odd sentences which he wrote, in this order, among other notes on the back of Watson's dignified title-page.

> To defend the Bible in this year 1798 would cost a man his life.
> But to him who sees this mortal pilgrimage in the light that I see it, Duty to his country is the first consideration & safety the last.
> I have been commanded from Hell not to print this, as it is what our Enemies wish.   383

In face of Bishop Watson's Heaven, Blake is, of course, quoting Hell as a giver of good advice. Its advice settles the to-and-fro of these three sentences of debate, and settles it against printing. Was the reason given with the advice, 'as it is what our Enemies wish', really just? Did the enemies of the Revolution really wish to provoke its friends to come into the open, as Lady Malmesbury had wished:

> As for Fox and Grey, I wish they would utter treason at once and be beheaded and hanged.

There is a letter written by Pitt in this year, 1798, which shows that the Government could lay fairly long trains of provocation.

> There is a strong feeling among many of our friends that some decided notice must be taken of Fox's speech. An idea has been suggested which I think deserves consideration. It is to begin with one of the measures we talked of, that of ordering him to attend. If he disavows, prosecuting the printer. If he avows, ordering him to be reprimanded, and then (which is the new part of the suggestion) if he offers a fresh insult at the next Whig Club, instead of gratifying him by an expulsion to send him to the Tower for the remainder of the session.

This from the Prime Minister in a year of war, famine, and financial crisis, is leisurely and statesman-like. The Government was about to attack the London Corresponding Society afresh. Ironically, the Act which suppressed the Society next year stands in the Statute Book on one side, and the Combination Laws stand on the other side, of an Act to regulate the slave trade more humanely. Habeas Corpus was again suspended, and there were fresh attacks on the Press: 'prosecuting the printer'. This was the year in which the anonymity of the newspaper was ended.

Yet what had Blake to fear, had he printed his notes openly over his own name? We can answer this question. Three well-known men attacked Richard Watson's renegade writings. One was William Wordsworth, in his *Letter to the Bishop of Llandaff* of 1793. Like Blake, Wordsworth charged Watson with conspiring against the friends of the Revolution:

> Left to the quiet exercise of their own judgment, do you think that the people would have thought it necessary to set fire to the house of the philosophic Priestley?

He charged Watson with perverting the pity which men had felt for the suffering people of France before the Revolution, by turning that pity to her king and her priests. Like Blake, Wordsworth saw Watson 'aim an arrow at liberty and philosophy, the eyes of the human race'. The second to attack Watson was Blake. The third was the scholar Gilbert Wakefield, who answered an *Address* by Watson in 1798 in his *Reply to the Bishop of Llandaff*. Neither Wordsworth nor Blake printed their attacks, and both remained free all their lives. Wakefield printed his, and was imprisoned for it from 1799 to 1801. And in this year 1798, Joseph Johnson himself was at last trapped and imprisoned, precisely for selling a copy of Wakefield's *Reply to the Bishop of Llandaff* to an *agent provocateur*. We may think Blake overwrought, and his fears a little mad. 'To defend the Bible in this year 1798 would cost a man his life' is an overstatement. But what grows striking, as we learn of the prosecutions of others, is how shrewdly Blake judged the temper of these years. The silences, the obscurities, the mumbling code names of the books which follow *The French Revolution* are those of a mystic with a harsh understanding of the world in which he was forced to live: in which he knew himself to be a rebel, and in which he felt himself a prisoner.

SEVEN

After *The French Revolution* Blake went back to the vague and mazy writing of *Tiriel*, because his world urged him there. But we must guard against the ready conclusions, that his world forced him there; that only the censor forced him there; and that the censor could have forced any man there. The censor never silenced Tom Paine, Gilbert Wakefield, and William Hone. Though the urge came from without, the caution and the secretiveness were within Blake, even in small matters: 'I did not tell him so plain & wish you to keep it a secret & to burn this letter because it speaks so plain'. The mind which thought in the smoky symbols of *Tiriel* was ready to go back to such symbols. We can only give reasons for believing that it might not have gone back, had it not felt it to be safer to go back. Nor did Blake's mind turn back from fear alone; it also turned back, from helplessness. Blake had belonged, as he said, to the Paine set. When he wrote *The French Revolution* the Paine set had known where were its sympathies and what were its hopes. But after 1792, when the Government began to break up the Paine set, its hopes were failing. And as the French crowd was drilled into the armies of Napoleon, its sympathies also wavered. There was a large shift of sympathy in England in 1797. It speaks for Blake's staunchness that he went on hating 'the English Crusade against France' long after. But, like other radicals, he was already baffled and hopeless. This is the state of mind which shaped and fills the prophetic books; and it makes them more baffling than do their secret names. For this makes puzzles which were not set for the censor: puzzles to which Blake himself knew no answers. Though his graver never rested, it no longer hoped to reach an end.

In Blake, Washington and Lafayette had of course always been symbolic figures, no more and no less personal than Los. Blake's prophetic books had not been history even when they had used historical names. But history had once given their symbolism a direction and a hope; and now it had neither.

It is not enough, therefore, to think of Blake's prophetic books without Blake. And neither is it enough to think of them without Blake's world. That world was wider than its censorship. But it was a world of censorship. It was the world of the acts against Seditious Writings, against Seditious Meetings, against Seditious Societies, against Treasonable Practices. It was the world of prosecutions for blasphemy, and of the laws against cheap newspapers. It was the world of the Militia Bills and of the Combination Laws. It was Pitt's world. That world did not make Blake; but it baffled him, and cowed him. Blake remained free all his life. But he was once tried for sedition.

THE SATANIC WHEELS

Machines

ONE

In 1789 the novelist Fanny Burney, who later married an exiled French general, was Second Keeper of the Robes to the Queen. Speaking with Lord Mountmorres, she was shocked to hear him fear that revolutionary feeling would now come to England. Her friends Samuel Johnson and Edmund Burke had praised English law with such assurance that she could think of no cause for discontent. 'In what could be its pretence?' she asked. Lord Mountmorres answered, 'The game laws, and the tithes.'

It was the common view, and it long remained so. Distress grew, and discontent became frightening; plainly, those among whom they grew were poor; and to the 'people thoroughly frightened', Lord Grenville's 'body of landed gentlemen in this country', the poor were village poor. Therefore country magistrates spent £2,000,000 in poor relief in 1792, more than £4,000,000 in 1802, more than £7,000,000 in 1813. Their relief did little to meet industrial distress. The squires and the Commons had hardly heard of factory workers. The North Country men about Pitt knew better; and Pitt had begun to take measures in 1792, on the plea that

> A spirit had appeared in some of the manufacturing towns which made it necessary that troops should be kept near them.

But Pitt had taken his measures first, and asked Parliament after. Only in 1799 did William Wilberforce press Parliament to turn a Bill, meant to control the workers in one trade, into the laws forbidding all Combinations of workmen.

We cannot wonder that the growth of industry took so long to become common knowledge. The steps by which industry had moved from the village to the factory had been small, scattered, secret, in little-known techniques. They were steps by which industry drew together; and they had taken it to places so far from London that even their names seemed outlandish. No Government had thought of taxing the new manufactures until 1784, when the Government tried to tax their raw stuffs. Since the industrial towns had no seats in Parliament, the great Midland manufacturers had to lobby the Whig Opposition. These Midland dissenters who had grown up in their workshops, the potter Wedgwood, the ironmaster Wilkinson, the engine-maker Boulton, held longest from Tory fears. After the Birmingham riot of 1791, they raised a subscription for Joseph Priestley. In 1794 the Marquis of Stafford warned Boulton 'that the country was upon the brink of a ruinous attempt to overthrow its Constitution', by the London Corresponding Society. But Matthew Boulton felt that the country was rather safer than one of his engineers. The warning which he passed to his partner James Watt was,

> I hope to God our Southerns is out of the mess, & that none of his letters will be found amongst these papers, & I wish you would speak to him about it, for I have reasons for my fears & wish to guard him.

TWO

The steps which took industry to its own revolution are now plainer. The village workmen could remain masters only so long as they could buy their raw stuffs. They could buy their raw stuffs only so long as they could sell their manufactures. When the price of manufactures slumped, the small masters had to borrow. And the price of manufactures often slumped: it slumped whenever war narrowed the export market: and England was at war for more than half of the eighteenth century. The small masters borrowed raw stuffs, and became workers for a putting-out merchant. They borrowed on their tools, and came to rent them from an owning merchant. Before Blake was born, most weavers, stocking-knitters, nailmakers, and others had already lost their small capital. Many had lost their tools, and were selling only their labour. The threshold to ownership was growing too high, even before the coming of the factory.

The merchants and middlemen who had bought out these men had wanted to run industry: they had not set out to own it. But now that they had sunk capital in raw stuffs and tools, they could keep up profits on this capital only by using it fully. They must rationalize industry. The worker at home did not give the best return. He was careless with stuffs and tools which he did not own; he was idle when he had earned his keep; having little hope of becoming a master, he was thriftless. He was still suffered to stay at home, because there he had the help of his family. As soon as greater help was offered by drawing industry together, by breaking its processes into unskilled linked steps, and by working its machines by power, he was moved to the factory. With these means Arkwright made his spinneries great, and Boulton his metal-works. The means of rationalization: the machine and the factory; the ring, the cartel, and the trust: these were not new. But in Blake's lifetime they became the norms of industry; and Blake knew their purpose.

> Wheel without wheel,
> To perplex youth in their outgoings & to bind to labours in
>   Albion
> Of day & night the myriads of eternity: that they may grind
> And polish brass & iron hour after hour, laborious task,
> Kept ignorant of its use: that they might spend the days of
>   wisdom
> In sorrowful drudgery to obtain a scanty pittance of bread.   700

The industries best fitted to gain by factory methods were those making textiles. Of these, the woollen industry was heavily protected; and rationalization was therefore pressed in the rival cotton industry. Both industries had unbounded markets in Europe, in America, and in Africa. In both, the skilled and well-paid weaver had outpaced the casual spinster, who spun only to eke out farm wages. For twenty-five years before Blake's birth, weaving was being speeded up: for example, by the use of a mechanical shuttle, at least in the cotton industry; and there had been a growing shortage of yarn. Two inventions of the 1760s righted the balance. One was the many-spindled jenny of James Hargreaves, in which the spindles themselves stretched and twisted the thread which they were winding. The other was the frame patented by Richard Arkwright, which spun the thread as it were with mechanical fingers, by drawing it through rollers each pair of which turned faster than the pair before it. By 1779, Samuel Crompton had made an invention which in effect married these two together, in a mule which is largely the spinning machine of to-day.

Arkwright had probably stolen his invention from the mechanic Thomas Highs; and it had been made by others before Highs, about 1736. But Arkwright turned this and kindred inventions into real power machines; he organized the machines in factories; and he did what the mechanics did not know how to do, he made the factories pay. Hitherto, English cotton cloths had had linen warps; and Parliament had protected these fustians against the pure cotton cloths of India, by forbidding the use of all pure cotton cloths. It was Arkwright's gift, not merely to spin a cotton thread strong enough to make warps, but to get Parliament to withdraw its laws against it. He got bankers and hosiers to back him; he bought his way into rival firms; when his patents were overthrown, he beat down his rivals without them. Vigorous, ambitious, ruthless, self-made, and with no past knowledge of his industry, he was the model of the new captains of the textile industry.

THREE

Like the woollen and the cotton industries, the English iron industry had long been held back by the shortage of one of its raw stuffs: charcoal to smelt and fine the plentiful iron ore. Once the Surrey ironmasters, who had enraged Queen Elizabeth by selling cannon to Navy and pirates alike, had made their charcoal in the oak scrub there.

> The Surrey hills glow like the clinkers of the furnace; Lambeth's Vale

> Where Jerusalem's foundations began, where they were laid in
>   ruins,
> Where they were laid in ruins from every Nation, & Oak
>   Groves rooted,
> Dark gleams before the Furnace-mouth a heap of burning
>   ashes.   485

Since then, the furnaces had moved west and north in search of charcoal. But charcoal probably remained scarce, and was certainly dear and awkward in use: for it is so easily crushed that iron ore could be smelted with it only a little at a time. In 1749 pig iron was so scarce that it had to be imported from America, in spite of the petition of the tanners of Sheffield and elsewhere.

> If the Bill should pass the English iron would be undersold; consequently a great number of furnaces and forges would be discontinued; in that case the woods used for fuel would stand uncut, and the tanners be deprived of oak bark sufficient for the continuation of their occupation.

A stronger and more plentiful stuff was needed to smelt iron ore. The stuff was coke, that is coal from which have been burnt off some of the impurities which make iron brittle and unworkable. It is not easy to use coke in smelting, for it must be done in a large furnace and with a strong blast. The process was tried by William Wood in 1726, after Swift had driven his halfpence out of Ireland. Swedenborg, then an expert in mining and metals, reported its failure. But the process had in fact been worked secretly since about 1709 by a family of Shropshire ironmasters, the Darbys. It had since been learnt by a neighbouring family, the Wilkinsons. Iron cast straight from the blast furnace began to take over many of the uses of fined wrought iron. It began to make new uses for itself, for example in the founding of engines. By 1762 the Darbys and the Wilkinsons were forming a ring to charge the same prices for their castings. The Darbys were already a vertical trust, feeding their furnaces from their own coal- and iron-mines. Ways were found by 1784 of stirring and rolling the dross out of iron also fined with coke, so that it could be wrought. But the stuff of the Industrial Revolution remained cast iron, the pride of John Wilkinson. By the 1790s, Matthew Boulton was minting Wilkinson's wage tokens, and they were good coin in every Shropshire iron town. The iron-masters were masters of the West Country. It is pleasant to know that the artless tanners were also saved. In 1765, the *Society for the Encouragement of Arts, Manufactures, and Commerce* gave a prize of £100 to a poor country tanner, who had discovered how to tan with oak sawdust in place of bark.

FOUR

The two great industries of the Industrial Revolution, cotton and iron, and the many lesser industries, Birmingham chemicals and knick-knacks, Sheffield tools, Staffordshire china, shared two needs. They needed transport. This need was met by building, in the first thirty-five years of Blake's life, a network of better roads and new canals. And they needed coal, for their own use and for the use of their town-dwelling workmen, who could no longer cut fuel on the common. To meet this growing need, the coalminer had to work deeper seams. There, he had to face greater risks of falls and of gas. The Newcastle papers were hushing up pit explosions when Blake was still a child. And he had now always to face water.

Before Elizabethan times, miners in Europe had learnt that no suction pump will raise water much more than thirty feet, however powerful it is made. When Blake was born, most coal- and metal-mines were already working at depths of two hundred feet and more. They had therefore to be kept dry by sets of pumps working one above the other. Such a set of pumps needed an engine to work it; and the steam engines were invented, either as mining pumps themselves or to work mining pumps in this way. For most of the eighteenth century the mines used the engine of Thomas New-comen, a West Country smith and engineer. In this engine the piston was raised by steam, and fell back into the vacuum made when a jet of water condensed the steam; its rise and fall worked the pump rods. Using steam only just above air pressure, the en-gine was little more than a suction engine; and was plainly modelled on the suction pump. But it worked, so long as the rush of water was not great. And unlike an earlier engine by Thomas Savery modelled on the force pump, and unlike many force pumps, it did not regularly blow itself to pieces.

Newcomen's engine was used in coal-mines, because the coal which it used cost nothing there. But it was hopelessly wasteful elsewhere, because the cylinder was chilled at each stroke, and much of the steam on the next stroke went to reheat it. When Boulton made the round of the Cornish copper-mines about 1775, he found that of the forty engines there 'there are only eighteen of 'em in work on account of ye high price of coal'. Boulton had then just begun an engine business with the instrument-maker James Watt, who had been at work since 1763 to remake the engine with a condensing chamber away from the cylinder. In this partnership Watt went on to drive the piston down by steam, as well as up; and to make it turn a factory wheel, in place of lifting a pump rod.

The story of Watt's engine is commonplace; but behind it stand two forces of the Industrial Revolution which are less well known. First, Watt made his engine work only under the press of precise needs. He had been toying with it for years, before he faced the tasks of making it in John Roebuck's coal-mines. Roebuck was feeding his great Carron ironworks from these mines, and his Newcomen engine had been overwhelmed by flooding. When Roebuck went bankrupt in the slump of 1772, Watt's new partner Boulton found for market the water-logged mines of Cornwall, where coal was so dear that they based the rent for their engine on its coal saving. Boulton and Watt even took shares in these mines in order to keep them open; and in 1785 Boulton and Josiah Wedgwood formed a Cornish copper cartel, to pool the market with the Anglesey surface mines. And Boulton in 1781 turned Watt to the new needs of the factories, then looking for a means to replace their feeble and uncertain water power.

> There is no other Cornwall to be found, and the most likely line for increasing the consumption of our engines is the application of them to mills which is certainly an extensive field.

> The people in London, Manchester and Birmingham are *steam mill mad*. I don't mean to hurry you, but I think that in the course of a month or two we should determine to take out a patent for certain methods of producing rotative motion.

it was in making these engines to turn a factory wheel that Watt fixed the horse-power in 1782, and Blake protested—

> The Villages Lament: they faint, outstretch'd upon the plain.
> Wailing runs round the Valleys from the Mill & from the
>   Barn.

> The Horse is of more value than the Man.   275

To prove the worth of their engine to the manufacturers 'steam mill mad', Boulton and Watt put it into the Albion flour mill in 1786. The grinding gear was John Rennie's first work in London. The Albion mill became a showplace, counted among the sights of London, until it was burned in 1791. This is how it came to be linked with the sorrows of Albion in Blake's mind.

> The living & the dead shall be ground in our rumbling Mills
> For bread of the Sons of Albion.   673

Second, Watt could not save Roebuck, because the Scottish smiths could not make engine parts with the precision needed to make his engine work. And Watt took Boulton for partner because only in Boulton's workshops had he seen this precision. The engine could hardly have worked then, had not John Wilkinson just invented a way of boring cylinders true. Watt's thoughts became engines in the hands of self-taught mechanics such as William Murdock, self-reliant, inventive, and precise. Their workmanship then made the high-pressure engine of the Cornish engineer Richard Trevithick, about 1800. The Industrial Revolution moved by the skill of its mechanics. It moved from what the engineer asked to what the mechanic could make, from what the mechanic made to what the engineer might plan. Its horror was that the mechanic's skill commonly threw him out of work.

FIVE

In 1793 one of Arkwright's more humane partners finished the building of a new spinning-mill. He kept one of the mechanics who had built it, as an odd-job man at 12s. a week. There was no other place for a man in the mill. There were places for the odd-job man's wife and four children: they earned the greater part of the family's wage, another 15s. a week.

1 A page from Blake's Notebook, including a self-portrait

Fiery the Angels rose, & as they rose deep thunder r
Around their shores; indignant burning with the fires of
And Bostons Angel cried aloud as they flew thro' the

He cried; Why trembles honesty and like a murderer
Why seeks he refuge from the frowns of his immortal s
Must the generous tremble & leave his joy, to the idle
    the pestilence!
That mock him? who commanded this? what God? what A
To keep the genrous from experience till the ungenerous
Are unrestraind performers of the energies of nature
Till pity is become a trade, and generosity a science
That men get rich by, & the sandy desert is givn to the s
What God is he, writes laws of peace, & clothes him in a te
What pitying Angel lusts for tears, and fans himself with
What crawling villain preaches abstinence & wraps him
In fat of lambs? no more I follow, no more obedience pa

2 **A page** from an early Prophetic Book, *America*, page 11

From Golgonooza the spiritual Four fold London eternal
In immense labours & sorrows, ever building, ever falling,
Thro Albions four Forests which overspread all the Earth:
From London Stone to Blackheath east: to Hounslow west:
To Finchley north: to Norwood south: and the weights
Of Enitharmons Loom play lulling cadences on the
        winds of Albion
From Caithness in the north, to Lizard-point & Dover in the south

Loud sounds the Hammer of Los, & loud his Bellows is heard
Before London to Hampsteads breadths & Highgates heights To
Stratford & old Bow: & across to the Gardens of Kensington
On Tyburns Brook: loud groans Thames beneath the iron Forge
Of Rintrah & Palamabron of Theotorm & Bromion: to
        forge the instruments
Of Harvest: the Plow & Harrow to pass over the Nations

The Surrey hills glow like the clinkers of the furnace: Lambeths Vale
Where Jerusalems foundations began: where they were laid in ruins
Where they were laid in ruins from every Nation & Oak Groves rooted
Dark gleams before the Furnace-mouth a heap of burning ashes
When shall Jerusalem return & overspread all the Nations
Return: return to Lambeths Vale O building of human souls
Thence stony Druid Temples overspread the Island white
And thence from Jerusalems ruins, from her walls of salvation
And praise: thro the whole Earth were reard from Ireland
To Mexico & Peru west, & east to China & Japan: till Babel
The Spectre of Albion frownd over the Nations in glory & war
All things begin & end in Albions ancient Druid rocky shore
But now the Starry Heavens are fled from the mighty limbs of
        Albion

armies

Loud sounds the Hammer of Los, loud turn the Wheels of Enith-
Her Looms vibrate with soft affections, weaving the Web of Life
Out from the ashes of the Dead; Los lifts his iron Ladles
With molten ore: he heaves the iron cliffs in his rattling chains
From Hyde Park to the Alms-houses of Mile-end & old Bow
Here the Three Classes of Mortal Men take their fixd destinations
And hence they overspread the Nations of the whole Earth & hence
The Web of Life is woven: & the tender sinews of life created
And the Three Classes of Men regulated by Los's Hammer. and
        woven

3   A page from a late Prophetic Book, *Milton*, page 4

4 The figures of Los, Enitharmon, and Orc, from *the First Book of Urizen*, page 19

5   The figure of Urizen or the Ancient of Days, from *Europe*, Frontispiece

6 A page from *Songs of Innocence* (later transferred), 'The Little Girl Found'

7 A page from *Songs of Experience*, 'The Chimney Sweeper'

8 Chained figures from *Visions of the Daughters of Albion*,
   Frontispiece

9   The Crucifixion

10   The Accusers, or Our End is Come

11   Hecate

12 The Wise and Foolish Virgins

13   The Ascent of the Mountain, from *Dante's Purgatorio*

14   The Morning Stars Singing Together, from *Job*

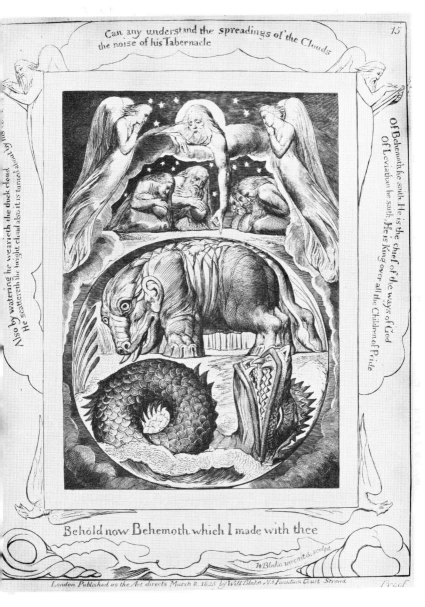

Can any understand the spreadings of the Clouds
the noise of his Tabernacle

15

Of Behemoth he saith He is the chief of the ways of God
Of Leviathan he saith, He is King over all the Children of Pride

Also by watering he wearieth the thick cloud
He scattereth the bright cloud also as it is turned about by his ....

Behold now Behemoth which I made with thee

W Blake invenit & sculpt

London Published as the Act directs March 8. 1825 by Will Blake N³ Fountain Court Strand

Proof

15   Behemoth, from *Job*

16   The Simoniac Pope, from *Dante's Inferno*

There was nothing new in a man's family eking out his earnings. Even in the golden 1720s Defoe had granted that the farmworker's wife and children must spin and card, if the family were not to 'fare hard, and live poorly'. Weavers now liked to recall those days, when a man could earn 10s. a week at the loom, his two sons 8s. each, and each had kept six hands or more spinning at 1s. or 2s. a week. I quote the dry comment: that this patriarchal family had to number twenty-one, in order to earn 60s. a week. The village worker on the farm and at the loom had always lived near the brink of hunger, and had been kept above it by his children's pennies a day. It is the burden of Defoe's delight: 'hardly any thing above four years old, but its hands are sufficient to it self.'

Nevertheless, the Whig age had kept the village worker above the brink. The Industrial Revolution shifted the balance sharply. The wife and children who had eked out the family wage now earned the greater part of it. Half the workers in the cotton mills were children; and of the other half, two-thirds were women. Their working day was fifteen hours, and in it they walked twenty miles among the machines. The elder Peel's Act of 1802 won a twelve-hour day only for parish children. By then, the steam mills were moving into the towns, where free children were plentiful. It was 1819 before he won a twelve-hour day for free children. And both Acts were for long mere paper Acts. Meanwhile, the fathers at the loom struggled on in a dying craft, whose wages began to fall after 1800 to less than a shilling a day. Others, among them most of the metalworkers, were left hopelessly behind by rising prices.

> Because of the Opressors of Albion in every City & Village.
> They mock at the Labourer's limbs: they mock at his starv'd
>   Children:
> They buy his Daughters that they may have power to sell his
>   Sons:
> They compell the Poor to live upon a crust of bread by soft
>   mild arts:
> They reduce the Man to want, then give with pomp & cere-
>   mony:
> The praise of Jehovah is chaunted from lips of hunger & thirst. 656

During Blake's life, the cost of living roughly doubled: wages went up roughly by one-half. The gap had to be filled by hunger, or by a new spurt of work from wife and children. And this gap does not count a loss which we can no longer measure: the loss of common rights.

The village worker on the farm and at his craft had hitherto kept some animals on the common, and had there cut his fuel. The village smallholders had farmed their land together, in strips. New ways of farming and of raising stock, and the dearth of corn, made these uses wasteful. The strips must be run together, and the common enclosed. In Blake's lifetime, Parliament passed Acts for more than three thousand enclosures. They would have been wise Acts, had they also safeguarded those whom they dispossessed. Instead, they gave them into the hands of the large owner and large buyer. *The Deserted Village* of Oliver Goldsmith is a newly enclosed village, although it wrongly describes enclosure upside down; it makes the usual error of the town-dweller of the time, in thinking that the encloser wanted to turn the village into a private park. Blake was following Goldsmith and Crabbe when he attacked

> The fat fed hireling with hollow drum,
> Who buys whole corn fields into wastes, and sings upon the
> heath.
> 193

For even the smallholder who could prove his claim to a holding could seldom pay to drain and fence it, and had to sell out. The farm-worker and the craftsman had no claim, for they held common rights only by custom; and they had no redress but riot. We can read the story of the villages in the words of Sir William Meredith to Parliament in 1772:

> That he once passing a Committee-room, when only one Member was holding a Committee, with a clerk's boy, he happened to hear something of hanging; he immediately had the curiosity to ask what was going forward in that small Committee that could merit such a punishment? He was answered, that it was an Inclosing Bill, in which a great many poor people were concerned, who opposed the Bill; that they feared those people would obstruct the execution of the Act, and therefore this clause was to make it capital felony in anyone who did so.

We have only hints to tell us what these rights to grazing and to fuel from the common had been worth. With them, the cottager's family in the Whig age had lived on less than 1s. 6d. a day, and the widow had lived on 2s. a week. Without them, they could not live at all: every workhouse in that age had failed, because its poor could not earn enough to keep themselves. But the plainest hint is given by the pamphlets on behalf of enclosure, which urge it as a blessing that, no longer able to fall back on the common, 'the labourers will work every day in the year'. This is the ground on which Samuel Johnson, who held that a man with money 'cannot make a bad use of his money, so far as regards Society', said of the man without money:

> Raising the wages of day-labourers is wrong; for it does not make them live better, but only makes them idler, and idleness is a very bad thing for human nature.

And it is the ground on which the owners of industry argued that, since the poor 'will never work any more time in general than is necessary just to live and support their weekly debauches',

> we can fairly aver that a reduction of wages in the woollen manufacture would be a national blessing and advantage, and no real injury to the poor.

The new farming, like the factory, needed a source of steady labour; and the enclosures found it. Before Blake died, William Cobbett said bitterly that the farm-worker had been driven upon piece-work.

The pamphlets assured the worker and the smallholder that, in the time which he had spent on common and holding, he would earn enough to buy more fuel, food, and clothing than he had got from them. Nevertheless, he feared that, once he had lost his rights, he would have to work for what wage was given. He would have to buy fuel, food, and clothing at what price was asked. And he was not sure that the two would meet. Adam Smith had indeed just proved that they must meet. And Burke, in his *Thoughts on Scarcity*, was at pains to rewrite Adam Smith for the farm-worker.

> In the case of the farmer and the labourer, their interests are always the same, and it is absolutely impossible that their free

contracts should be onerous to either party. It is the interest of the farmer that his work should be done with effect and celerity; and that cannot be, unless the labourer is well fed, and otherwise found with such necessaries of animal life, according to his habitudes, as may keep the body in full force, and the mind gay and cheerful.

Unhappily, the farmer read neither Adam Smith nor Burke. Even before the French wars, wages were falling short of prices. In 1795 there was talk of drawing up a new Poor Law. Instead, that year the magistrates at Speenhamland in Berkshire made a fatal innovation in the Poor Law: they used it to make up farm wages to a sum to keep pace with the price of bread. Their scale spread through the South Country; the farmer paid less, and the rates doled out more; and the man who had been a worker and a smallholder became the hanger-on of the parish. The rates rose frighteningly, and were paid, avowedly, only for fear of revolution. This rise, and this fear, are the background to the pessimism of the Reverend Thomas Robert Malthus's well-known *Essay on the Principle of Population* of 1798, in mockery of which Blake wrote angrily:

> When a man looks pale
> With labour & abstinence, say he looks healthy & happy;
> And when his children sicken, let them die; there are enough
> Born, even too many, & our Earth will be overrun
> Without these arts.
> Preach temperance: say he is overgorg'd & drowns his wit
> In strong drink, tho' you know that bread & water are all
> He can afford.
>
> 323

SIX

English farmers and manufacturers alike were making huge profits throughout the French wars. Why, then, did Governments allow them so grossly to mishandle wages, alike in farming and in industry?

It is fair to begin the answer by reminding ourselves that few men and no Governments understood the changes which the Industrial Revolution was then making. Even the men who understood them, of whom Blake was one, had no notion how they could be handled. Farming was old, and in England industry was as old. Both had paid traditional wages for more than a hundred years: a shilling a day, up to two shillings for skilled work. There had been no striking rise in prices until Blake was born, since the great gold inflation of Elizabethan times. It was easy to think that the balance between owner and worker, which had been righting itself with less and less Government check, would go on doing so. This was the Whig view of Locke, Petty, and Mandeville, that self-interest would right every unbalance: *let be*. It had been enlarging English trade for a hundred years. And, in 1776, Adam Smith had given this view a reasoned setting in *The Wealth of Nations*. It was natural that Ministers, bewildered and overwhelmed, should grasp at this proof that they had best do nothing. Faced by the unbelievable growth, which they would not believe, of manufacturers and of workmen, they were glad to think that 'it is absolutely impossible that their free contracts should be onerous to either party'.

There were opposition voices. Samuel Whitbread argued in Parliament that no contract was free so long as the Combination Laws, in effect, hampered only one party. But when Whitbread spoke, the French Revolution had long given another force to *let be*. Helpless to handle industrial change, Governments had grown to fear every change: 'I am frightened at the consequences of any innovation upon a long-established practice, at a period so full of dangers as the present'. Whitbread's reasoning was good, but it was not helpful, when Governments feared precisely that workmen might become too strong a party. They feared revolution; and owners were free to cash their fear. The policy of helplessness, *let be*, had become the policy of terror, *let us be*. There is no mistaking Wilberforce's words:

> The circumstance which rendered our militia so dear to us, as a constitutional force, was its being officered by country gentlemen—men of property, of family, of domestic connections, of personal influence, whose arms were in no conjuncture likely to be turned against their country.

This change of policy is as marked in Pitt as in Wilberforce. In Pitt's finances the helplessness is uppermost. He did not understand the new industries. He even starved them of small change, so that owners had to coin their own trade and wage tokens from 1787. He did not know how to tax them. At a time of growing profits, he let six years of war go by before he began an income tax in 1799. Before this, his borrowing had already broken credit, and the Bank of England's gold had run out. The National Debt, swollen by two costly wars since 1756, grew more than threefold during the French wars, to £800,000,000. Pitt's borrowing had included, fantastically, money at high interest for a sinking fund, to pay off debts on which the State was paying a lower interest. England was living by inflation.

This helplessness was not Pitt's alone. George III would not have taken a man of twenty-three, and a Pitt, for Chancellor of the Exchequer in 1782, had not others felt helpless. Parliament would not have taken Pitt all his life for a financial wonder, had it not felt helpless. It would not otherwise have agreed to the sinking-fund scheme, which Pitt was known to have taken from Richard Price. Tom Paine believed that Pitt had gone to the second part of *The Rights of Man* for financial advice. Certainly Pitt took some of the advice. He and his Government did not learn from such men by choice, but because they knew themselves to be hard-pressed and helpless.

But the fear grew greater than the helplessness: one example will show how much greater. When the country was full of wage tokens, an informer wrote to Pitt about those of John Wilkinson:

> The Presbyterian tradesmen receive them in payment for goods, by which intercourse they have frequent opportunities to corrupt the principles of that description of men by infusing into their minds the pernicious tenets of Payne's *Rights of Man*.

Pitt was the tool of such fears, and has become their symbol. But we must not misjudge him, as if what happened in his short life—he died in 1806 at the age of forty-seven, having been Prime Minister for all but three years since 1783—had been a mere personal history. He was, personally, a secret and a hysterical man. He was weak and anxious, and by irresolution yielded to George III, and to his Party, Acts which a show of firmness would have carried. It was thus that he gave up every principle which had made him

a leader in Parliament: the reform of sinecures, of corruption, and
of the suffrage; toleration for dissenters, and for Roman Catholics;
the new Poor Law; even Wilberforce's Bills against slavery, which
Fox carried in six months of office when Pitt died. Pitt yielded his
principles to his coalitions, because he believed that the coalition
of property had become more urgent than principle. The leader of
this coalition had needs to speak its lowest common language, and
to become the mind within Tory reaction, the will of George III
sane and mad. The greatest of the Whig gamblers, Charles James
Fox, who was a professional politician, at times in the worst meaning, could remain steadfast in his principles: he knew no greater
loyalty. But even Whigs came to feel another loyalty, and to see in
their party, as Burke did,

> the party in its composition and in its principles connected
> with the solid, permanent, long-possessed property of the
> country.

Others held to the loyalty to property from other motives: Adding-
ton and Castlereagh from habit, Eldon from self-interest, and
Canning cynically from ambition. But Pitt held to it honestly,
because his world rested on property, and because he believed that
the threat to property threatened the world. Unhappily, as Blake
saw, not motives but 'acts themselves alone are history'. Byron said
what was to be said for George III:

> I grant his household abstinence, I grant
> His neutral virtues, which most monarchs want;
> I know he was a constant consort; own
>   He was a decent sire and middling lord,
> All this is much, and most upon a throne.

And the lines with which Byron ends this list remain apt to William Pitt the younger:

> I grant him all the kindest can accord:
> And this was well for him, but not for those
> Millions who found him what oppression chose.

For the loyalty to property became a nightmare to England. Nothing came to weigh in policy but fear of the Revolution. In the
dearth of 1795 the Government had forbidden the making of hair-
powder. The loss turned out to be small, for the powder tax never

reached the £250,000 which had been hoped for it. Six years later, in the greatest dearths in English history, it was taken for granted that the making of hair-powder would again be forbidden. But George Rose, the mouthpiece of Pitt, wrote to Wilberforce:

> We did prohibit the distillation of wheat; and allowed the importation of starch at the Home Duty, which will stop that manufactory; but I deplore most sincerely and earnestly any agreement against the use of hair powder, not merely for the sake of a large revenue, but to avoid other mischief which I am very sure is not enough attended to, the distinction of dress and external appearance. The inattention to that has been a great support of Jacobinism.

SEVEN

Until the peace of 1802 the policy of fear seldom went beyond politics. The attacks were made mainly on radical writers and on reform clubs. There were men in the Government who believed that they saw farther: who chose, among reform clubs, those at a penny a week, and who feared the Combinations of workmen. They had read the stories of spies, and the secret report which, in 1792, feared that the sympathy of the militiamen with the poor made it

> a dangerous measure to keep troops in the manufacturing Towns in their present dispersed state, and unless Barracks could be established for them where they could be kept under the eyes of their officers it would be prudent to Quarter them in the towns and villages in the vicinity.

But the landed Commons learned to share these larger fears, only when they learned of the industrial poor. Only then, about the beginning of the new Napoleonic war in 1803, did the fear of radicalism become openly a fear of working-men.

The shift was made easier by the change between the two French wars. The war of 1793–1802 had begun as a war against the French Revolution. The rise of Napoleon in 1796, to First Consul in 1799, had estranged many liberals from France. Nevertheless, they rightly felt that the Government was prolonging the war as a crusade against freedom. When Fox went to Paris in 1802, he thought, and may have spoken, of 'Liberty being *asleep* in France but *dead* in

England'. But from 1803, and after Napoleon made himself Emperor in 1804, there was no doubt that the new war was being fought against an imperial France. The threat of invasion was real at the beginning of this war; and it did what such threats must do, even when they are real; as Jonathan Swift knew, eighty years before this:

> Perhaps a *seasonable Report of some Invasion would have been spread in the most proper Juncture*, which is a great Smoother of Rubs in Publick Proceedings; and we should have been told that *this was no Time to create Differences when the Kingdom was in Danger.*

The Opposition had to uphold the war: after Pitt died, Fox joined the Government for the last six months of his life. Therefore it did not feel free to embarrass the Government, and ceased to be an Opposition that must be reckoned with. It is the irony of just wars, that they leave only Governments free. Having no checks, the Governments of 1803–15 were able to build a reaction which dwarfed that of the war against the French Revolution. This is the reaction which lingered into the Holy Alliance, the Peterloo massacre, and the Six Acts.

This reaction was now aimed at working-men. The working-men were no longer moved by the hopes of the French Revolution, but by the hardships of inflation, high prices, low wages, the threats of hunger and of unemployment. To them, and to the Government, the war therefore became a war at home. Prosecutions grew under the Combination Laws, and under forgotten earlier laws. And more than prosecutions, their threat bred the secrecy, the terror, and the despair of the meetings on the moor, the storming of mills, King Ludd face to face with King Hunger. Pressed by Sheridan, the Government had amended the Combination Laws in 1800, so that they also forbade combinations of owners. They were not repealed until 1824, and then only for a short time. We can judge what their amendment was worth, when we learn that a secret committee of Nottingham hosiers had for its secretary the town clerk. It was he who hit on the notion of breaking the strike of frameworkers in 1814, not by using the doubtful militia, but by disbanding it in order to make more workless. About this time, the Admiralty assured Samuel Whitbread that the press gangs were not singling out political suspects, while *The Newcastle Chronicle* was writing:

Monday, near thirty riotous seamen were taken on the Tyne
at Shields and lodged safe in His Majesty's ship *Transit*. The
peace of this port has frequently been disturbed, under pretence of demanding more wages; but now positive orders are
given by the Admiralty to the commanding officer here to
impress such lawless hands and send them to the Nore.

The Industrial Revolution had made a new plenty. Farming and
industry alike were booming. There was work for men at any
number of machines, had it been given them at a living wage. Not
the machines were breaking the men, but their owners. And the
men broke the machines because they belonged to owners. So
London knitters and silk-weavers had broken machines throughout
the eighteenth century, whenever there had been wage quarrels. Of
the machine breakers of the Napoleonic war, only those of Yorkshire accused the new shearing frames of throwing men out of
work. Machine breaking in Lancashire grew out of bread riots, and
was started by *agents provocateurs*. The Nottingham Luddites, who
had begun the movement in 1811, broke the frames of owners who
were cutting wages. In the new economy of plenty, these men asked
to live by their work, not to starve by that of their wives and children. Like owners and Governments, like soldiers and learned men,
these men were helpless in the storm of the Industrial Revolution:
but they were hungrier, and hunted.

> All the marks remain of the slave's scourge & tyrant's Crown,
> And of the Priest's o'ergorged Abdomen, & of the merchant's
>   thin
> Sinewy deception, & of the warrior's outbraving & thought-
>   lessness
> In lineaments too extended & in bones too strait & long.
> They shew their wounds: they accuse: they sieze the opressor;
>   howlings began
> On the golden palace, songs & joy on the desart; the Cold babe
> Stands in the furious air; he cries: 'the children of six thousand
>   years
> Who died in infancy rage furious: a mighty multitude rage
>   furious,
> Naked & pale standing in the expecting air, to be deliver'd.'   363

The Satanic Wheels

ONE

On 11 January 1804, at Chichester Quarter Sessions—

> William Blake, an engraver at Felpham, was tried on a charge
> exhibited against him by two soldiers for having uttered sedi-
> tious and treasonable expressions.

Some of the words put into Blake's mouth by the two soldiers,
Scholfield and Cock, were fairly silly. They were said to have been
spoken when Blake had thrown Scholfield out of his garden. But it
was plain that what had rankled was the throwing out. Nevertheless, the charge was a grave charge, as Blake had learnt when it
was first made.

> I have been before a Bench of Justices at Chichester this
> morning; but they, as the Lawyer who wrote down the Accusa-
> tion told me in private, are compell'd by the Military to suffer
> a prosecution to be enter'd into: altho' they must know, & it
> is manifest, that the whole is a Fabricated Perjury. I have been
> forced to find Bail,   827

in the large sum of £250.

> It has struck a consternation thro' all the Villages round. Every
> Man is now afraid of speaking to, or looking at, a Soldier.
> Every one here is my Evidence for Peace & Good Neighbour-
> hood; & yet, such is the present state of things, this foolish
> accusation must be tried in Public.   828

The Quarter Sessions was headed by Charles Lennox, third Duke
of Richmond: that Duke whose Suffrage Bill had been before the

House of Lords when the Gordon rioters reached it in 1780. He had long joined Pitt's Government, an indifferent Master of Ordnance, with a name for saving his pocket at the public's cost. Peter Pindar, in his satires, was fond of coupling him with Pitt, as two reformers whose zeal had carried them into office but had not followed them there. The leaders of the London Corresponding Society, at their trial in 1794, had made much of a letter on Parliamentary reform which the Duke of Richmond had written in his zealous days, and had called him as a witness. This scandal had forced him out of office in 1795; and it had not endeared radicals to him. Now, at Blake's trial, he put his loyalty beyond doubt. Blake's counsel had to vie with him and to protest Blake's devotion to 'the sacred person of the sovereign', just then mad again. Hayley had not put his hopes higher than that the charge 'will at least be thrown out by the Court as groundless and vexatious'. Blake was lucky to be wholly cleared by the jury.

The charge had come at a grave time for Blake. In 1793 Blake had moved to poorer lodgings in Lambeth, to a neighbourhood of decayed pleasure gardens and almshouses not far from *The Dog and Duck*, and near St George's Fields. Alas, the romantic highwaymen were now gone; during the famine years when Blake lived here, *The Dog and Duck* became a soup kitchen and made bread from potato flour. For seven years Blake went on working hard; and he went on finding it harder to make a living. Towards 1800 he had to count a good deal on the patronage of Thomas Butts. This otherwise unknown man now bought about fifty pounds' worth of Blake's work in most years: some because he liked it, and more because he liked the Blakes. The year 1800 was one of the worst of all the years of hunger and high prices. In that year Flaxman found Blake work for William Hayley, gentleman of letters, liberal, and bore. The work grew, and Blake was urged to move near Hayley, to Felpham on the Sussex coast. Though the move saved him from the worst years in London, it left him to the patronage of Hayley.

The move was meant to give Blake a fresh start, away from Joseph Johnson and his radical friends. Richard Price and Mary Wollstonecraft had died; Priestley was in America; and Paine was about to go there, from France. Henry Fuseli, who had been Blake's link with these men, may now have been less anxious to be counted

among them. But William Godwin was still in London; so was
Joseph Johnson; so were the last outspoken men of the London
Corresponding Society, among them Hardy and Home Tooke.
Although Blake felt that Fuseli and Johnson now passed his work
over, his more careful friends were glad to have him move beyond
their reach. As soon as Blake was in Felpham, Thomas Butts wrote
to him frankly.

> Whether you will be a better Painter or a better Poet
> from your change of ways & means I know not, but this
> I predict, that you will be a better Man – excuse me, as
> you have been accustomed from friendship to do, but
> certain opinions imbibed from reading, nourish'd by in-
> dulgence, and rivetted by a confined Conversation, and which
> have been equally prejudicial to your Interest & Happiness,
> will now, I trust, disperse as a Daybreak Vapour, and you
> will henceforth become a Member of that Community of
> which you are at present, in the opinion of the Archbishop
> of Canterbury, but a Sign to mark the residence of dim in-
> credulity, haggard suspicion, & bloated philosophy.

Blake himself was aware that it was hoped to turn him to the
milder liberalism of Flaxman and Hayley. Hard times, and the
changes within France, had been puzzling him, and had begun to
cow him. On setting off for Felpham, he thanked Flaxman in lines
which pitifully speak his helplessness.

> I bless thee, O Father of Heaven & Earth, that ever I saw
>   Flaxman's face.
> Angels stand round my Spirit in Heaven, the blessed of
>   Heaven are my friends upon Earth.
> When Flaxman was taken to Italy, Fuseli was given to me
>   for a season,
> And now Flaxman hath given me Hayley his friend to be
>   mine, such my lot upon Earth.
>
> The American War began. All its dark horrors passed before
>   my face
> Across the Atlantic to France. Then the French Revolution
>   commenc'd in thick clouds,
> And My Angels have told me that seeing such visions I could
>   not subsist on the Earth,

> But by my conjunction with Flaxman, who knows to forgive
> Nervous Fear.   799

As Butts pointed out, this is not how Blake had spoken of Angels
in the past. The change was deliberate, to mark his acquiescence in
the new outlook which was planned for him. Humbly Blake wrote
to Butts, 'Dear Friend of My Angels' and 'Friend of Religion &
Order',

> Your prediction will, I hope, be fulfilled in me, & in future
> I am the determined advocate of Religion & Humility, the
> two bands of Society.   804

We need not set too great store by these resolutions of the
famine year 1800: Blake himself did not long do so. A year later,
he was writing thoughtlessly to Butts that he felt so light-hearted
that 'Bacon & Newton would prescribe ways of making the world
heavier to me, & Pitt would prescribe distress for a medicinal po-
tion'. These words would not please Butts and the Archbishop of
Canterbury. But when these words were written, it was known that
peace with France was in sight. The Preliminaries of Peace were
signed next month. There lay Blake's lightness of heart. No sooner
were the Preliminaries signed than Blake wrote to Flaxman:

> Now I hope to see the Great Works of Art, as they are so
> near to Felpham, Paris being scarce further off than London.
> But I hope that France & England will henceforth be
> as One Country and their Arts One, & that you will Ere long
> be erecting Monuments In Paris—Emblems of Peace.   811

Blake was not able to make the pilgrimage to Paris, which all
liberals who could made in the year of peace. Before peace was
formally signed in March 1802 he had begun to fall out with Hayley
and to be troubled about his future. He spent an uneasy year in
making up his mind to go back to London, however hard it might
be to find work there. And almost as soon as his mind was settled,
war began again in May 1803. The dilemma of loyalties which had
made Blake helpless in 1800 now mastered all liberals, and left
them unhappy and fearful as Blake had been then. Everyone must
rally against the threat of invasion, which was large all that year;
but would the Government therefore forget old scores? In August

803 there was a rumour that the French transports had set off, and all women etc.' were ordered away from the South coast. That month, Private John Scholfield brought his charges against William Blake.

TWO

Blake was tried on two charges. We need not trouble ourselves with he lesser, that Blake—

> did make an Assault and him the said John Scholfield then and there did beat and wound and ill treat so that his life was greatly despaired of and other wrongs to the said John Schol-field and against the Peace of our said Lord the King his Crown and Dignity.

There was little doubt that the jury would find Blake 'not Guilty of the Assault aforesaid'. The graver charge was—

> that on the Twelfth day of August in the Year of our Lord One thousand Eight hundred and three War was carrying on between the persons exercising the powers of Government in France and our said Lord the King, to wit, at the Parish of Felpham in the County of Sussex and That WILLIAM BLAKE late of the said Parish of Felpham ·in the said County of Sussex being a Wicked Seditious and Evil dis-posed person and greatly disaffected to our said Lord the King and Wickedly and Seditiously intending to bring our said Lord the King into great Hatred Contempt and Scandal with all his liege and faithful Subjects of this Realm and the Soldiers of our said Lord the King to Scandalize and Vilify and intending to withdraw the fidelity and allegiance of his said Majesty's Subjects from his said Majesty and to en-courage and invite as far as in him lay the Enemies of our said Lord the King to invade this Realm and Unlawfully and Wickedly to seduce and encourage his Majesty's Subjects to resist and oppose our said Lord the King.

Although this is one charge, it sets out two grounds against Blake. One is, that he wished to encourage and invite the Enemy to invade England. John Scholfield had deposed this, not alone of Blake but of his wife: 'Blake said, My Dear, you would not fight against France—she replyed no, I would for Bonaparte as long as I am able.' Had the trial been held in the invasion days of 1803, this might have been the larger ground. There is a hint, which might have been enlarged, of that part of the Act of 1795 against Treasonable Practices which made it high treason 'to move or stir any foreigner or stranger with force to invade this realm'. When the trial was held, in January 1804, the threat of invasion had grown slight. The court therefore took as ground that Blake had said—

> 'damn the King (meaning our said Lord the King) and Country (meaning this Realm) his Subjects (meaning the Subjects of our said Lord the King) and all you Soldiers (meaning the Soldiers of our said Lord the King) are sold for Slaves'.

The wording of the charge recalls another part of the Act against Treasonable Practices, which had made it high misdemeanour 'to excite or stir up the people to hatred or contempt of the person of his Majesty'. But it was the common wording of charges of sedition; and the court tried it as sedition. The jury's finding says precisely, 'William Blake is not Guilty of the Sedition aforesaid.'

The charge puts fairly what John Scholfield had deposed that Blake had said. The sum of that tirade had been, in Scholfield's words:

> If Bonaparte should come he would be Master of Europe in an Hour's Time, that England might depend upon it, that when he set his Foot on English Ground that every Englishman would have his choice whether to have his Throat cut, or to join the French, and that he was a strong Man, and would certainly begin to cut Throats, and the strongest Man must conquer – that he damned the King of England – his country, and his subjects, that his Soldiers were all bound for Slaves, and all the Poor People in general.

It is unlikely that Blake had said all this, and much more which Scholfield deposed. He would not have spoken thus of the French in 1803, even in the quarrel with Scholfield. It is unlikely that he ever spoke thus of Napoleon. Scholfield thought it a likely story for invasion days. But there is no doubt that Blake's solid village witnesses, who disliked the soldiers, would give the lie to the story.

But it is also unlikely that Blake had said none of this. The man who had written in the margin of Bacon's *Essays* 'Every Body hates a King!' could be moved to damn the king. And the gibe which rankled so that Scholfield recalled it twice, that soldiers are enslaved, chimes with Blake's beliefs. He believed this of 'all the Poor People in general', and grieved for it. If this was trumped up, it is at least odd that it should be so apt. Blake may not have said just this, on just this day. Scholfield may have heard gossip, that Blake and Hayley were not Church and King men. But Scholfield certainly knew how Blake sometimes spoke. The stress which he makes Blake give to the Weak and the Strong is that of Blake's own usage, and is uncommon. This is the stress with which Blake had written of England after the American revolt, that

> Weak men twelve years should govern o'er the strong;
> And then their end should come, when France reciev'd the
> Demon's light.   203

There is an odd truth in the claim which Scholfield put into Blake's mouth, that he had said such things to greater men. Although Hayley helped Blake through the trial, some of Hayley's greater friends believed Blake guilty.

We need not wonder that Blake, who knew something of Government informers, had written to Butts 'to learn somewhat about the Man' in London. Blake always believed that the Government had 'sent the soldier to entrap him' because he had belonged to the Paine set. He was needlessly afraid; the Chichester court seems to have known nothing of his past. Even had he been found guilty, he would therefore hardly have been sentenced to a very long term in prison. But it was as well that the court did not know Blake's past. Had it known it, we may doubt whether Blake would have gone free. We may doubt whether he would have gone free in London. And we may be sure that he would not have gone free in the manufacturing North.

THREE

The defeat of the French Revolution, the years of hardship, the move to Felpham, and the ambitions of Napoleon had ended Blake's hopes of a happy change. His trial frightened him away from all politics. The dilemma of liberalism, bound to uphold governments which were murdering it, revolted his conscience About 1810 Blake wrote the epitaph of his political hopes.

> I am really sorry to see my Countrymen trouble themselves about Politics. If Men were Wise, the Most arbitrary Princes could not hurt them. If they are not wise, the Freest Government is compell'd to be a Tyranny. Princes appear to me to be Fools. Houses of Commons & Houses of Lords appear to me to be fools; they seem to me to be something Else besides Human Life.   600

Years of greater hardship, for him and for England, had turned his hopes to despair. The men whom *The French Revolution* had praised, 'the fiery cloud of Voltaire, and thund'rous rocks of Rousseau', seemed to him to have planned only like those whom they had fought. All societies were planned within self-interest. Blake had no hope now but the self-destruction of society. He painted the patriot dead, Nelson and Pitt, as God's tools of anarchy, to destroy world and worldliness together. They are

> The Plow of Rintrah & the Harrow of the Almighty
> In the hands of Palamabron, Where the Starry Mills of Satan
> Are built beneath the Earth & Waters of the Mundane
>   Shell.   483

> The spiritual form of Pitt, guiding Behemoth; he is that Angel who, pleased to perform the Almighty's orders, rides on the whirlwind, directing the storms of war: He is ordering the Reaper to reap the Vine of the Earth, and the Plowman to plow up the Cities and Towers.   565

Blake had become a political quietist. He who had urged men to Energy now urged them 'to put off Self'. And he now wrote Angel and Satan as others used the words. When men change thus, they commonly also become social reactionaries. At this time, Wordsworth, Coleridge, and Southey had done so; Blake alone did not.

> Since the French Revolution Englishmen are all Intermeasurable One by Another, Certainly a happy state of Agreement to which I for One do not Agree.   878

Having grown to hate the wars of nations and of parties, he may even have come to see the social war more sharply. *Milton* and *Jerusalem* have put aside the symbols of England at war with America, and England at war with France. The symbol of the rich making war upon the poor is the plainer in them.

> A murderous Providence! A Creation that groans, living on Death,
> Where Fish & Bird & Beast & Man & Tree & Metal & Stone
> Live by Devouring.   681

In 1802 Humphry Davy had put the argument for a society at war within itself precisely.

> The unequal division of property and of labour, the differ-ence of rank and condition amongst mankind, are the sources of power in civilized life – its moving causes, and even its very soul.

Eight years later, in his notes on his *Vision of the Last Judgment*, Blake put the opposite argument, against the urge of poverty, as precisely.

> Poverty is the Fool's Rod, which at last is turn'd on his own back; this is A Last Judgment – when Men of Real Art Gov-ern & Pretenders Fall. Some People & not a few Artists have asserted that the Painter of this Picture would not have done so well if he had been properly Encourag'd. Let those who think so, reflect on the State of Nations under Poverty & their incapability of Art; tho' Art is Above Either, the Argument is better for Affluence than Poverty; & tho' he would not have been a greater Artist, yet he would have produc'd Greater works of Art in proportion to his means. A Last Judgment is not for the purpose of making Bad Men better, but for the Purpose of hindering them from opressing the Good with Poverty & Pain by means of Such Vile Arguments & Insinua-tions.   612

Eight years after this, Blake wrote the simple verses of *The Ever-lasting Gospel* against his society and its church, 'the Merchant Canaanite' and 'the rich learned Pharisee'. And nine years later, in 1827, Blake took up Dr Thornton's *New Translation of the Lord's Prayer*, and bitterly parodied one of its sentences thus:

> Give us day by day our Real Taxed Substantial Money bought
> Bread; deliver from the Holy Ghost whatever cannot be
> Taxed; for all is debts & Taxes between Caesar & us & one
> another.   78*

Against this, 'Doctor Thornton's Tory Translation', Blake put his
own forthright prayer.

> Give us the Bread that is our due & Right, by taking away
> Money, or a Price, or Tax upon what is Common to all in
> thy Kingdom.   788

These words are among the last which Blake wrote. He died that
summer. Blake had despaired of politics. But his social conscience
had not faltered in the Satanic years of the Corn Laws.

FOUR

The dark years, the Satanic mills: the furnace glare in the northern
sky, the glare of war to the south: these shoulder into, crowd, and
at last master Blake's later prophetic books.

> The Bellows are the Animal Lungs, the Hammers the Animal
>   Heart,
> The Furnaces the Stomach for Digestion; terrible their fury
> Like seven burning heavens rang'd from South to North.   684

Blake had written *Tiriel* about 1789; he did not finish *Jerusalem*
until about 1820. Although his prophetic books thus cover more
than thirty years, all the larger of them have a common theme.
Man is thwarted, and seeks to fulfil himself. He can find fulfilment
only in the experience of his works. But all works and all experience, by their nature, distort the vision to which they give shape,
and the self which they are to fulfil. Once again, therefore, man has
been thwarted. Once again he must try to break through the ring
which holds him from fulfilment, in the same cycle. This is the
endless treadmill of the prophetic books, cycle after cycle, and ring
beyond ring. The theme is the same, whether the fleeing symbol of
fulfilment is sexual in *The Book of Thel*, energetic in *The Book of
Urizen*, or religious in *Milton*. But as we go forward through these
books, we meet other changes which march together. There is a

change in the tyranny by which Blake sees man thwarted. The
blind monster Tiriel has given place, in *Jerusalem*, to 'The Looms
& Mills & Prisons & Work-houses of Og & Anak'. There is a change
in the slavery to which Blake sees man put. The crucified Fuzon of
The Book of Ahania, 'the pale living Corse on the Tree', becomes
Vala, mourning in a landscape of brick-making kilns which was
familiar round London.

> The King of Light beheld her mourning among the Brick
> kilns, compell'd
> To labour night & day among the fires; her lamenting voice
> Is heard when silent night returns & the labourers take their
> rest.
> 'O Lord, wilt thou not look upon our sore afflictions
> Among these flames incessant labouring? our hard masters
> laugh
> At all our sorrow. We are made to turn the wheel for water,
> To carry the heavy basket on our scorched shoulders, to sift
> The sand & ashes, & to mix the clay with tears & repentance.
> The times are now return'd upon us; we have given ourselves
> To scorn, and now are scorned by the slaves of our enemies.
> Our beauty is cover'd over with clay & ashes, & our backs
> Furrow'd with whips, & our flesh bruised with the heavy
> basket.'   285

And there is a change in the works which man must undertake, and
in the means by which they wrong the self which they seek to
fulfil. In place of Thel going among the flowers to the clay 'till to
her own grave plot she came' is Los at work at his furnaces until—

> When Los open'd the Furnaces before him
> He saw that the accursed things were his own affections
> And his own beloveds; then he turn'd sick: his soul died
> within him.   669

The theme has not changed. But in imagery and in imagination, we
are moving into a changed world. The world of *The Book of Urizen*
was one in which—

> Los encircled Enitharmon
> With fires of Prophecy
> From the sight of Urizen & Orc.
> And she bore an enormous race.   234

But the world of *Milton* is frankly that of the Industrial Revolution; and Los and Enitharmon have become symbols of that revolution.

> Loud sounds the Hammer of Los, loud turn the wheels of Enitharmon:
> Her Looms vibrate with soft affections, weaving the Web of Life
> Out from the ashes of the Dead; Los lifts his iron Ladles
> With molten ore: he heaves the iron cliffs in his rattling chains
> From Hyde Park to the Alms-houses of Mile-end & old Bow.
>
> 486

Los and Enitharmon had begun to play a growing part in the political books, and in the other books of 1794 and 1795, *The Book of Urizen, The Book of Ahania, The Book of Los*, and *The Song of Los*. But Los had rarely been given a hammer and forge, and there is only a hint that Enitharmon can weave. They first become main figures in *Vala or The Four Zoas*, written from 1795 to 1804, in some books of which Enitharmon is given a loom, and in which Los has his furnaces. Los and Enitharmon become the great industrial figures, master of the furnaces and mistress of the looms, in *Milton* and in *Jerusalem* after 1804.

This change is as marked in the stories in which these books tell their common theme. *Tiriel* had a vague story about a mountain chase; and the books of 1794 and 1795 went back to this chase. But the books written after 1795 tell always of the building of a city and a world. In *Vala or The Four Zoas*, the Mundane Shell is built. In *Milton* is built Golgonooza, a shadow London. And in *Jerusalem* is built the city which London and Golgonooza are to become, Jerusalem itself. These cities, symbols of states of man, are not the same. But they are symbols of the states of the man whom Blake knew, the town-dwelling and town-making man. And they shift always across the same state, that 'Golgonooza is nam'd Art & Manufacture by mortal men'. Golgonooza is the London of the *Society for the Encouragement of Arts, Manufactures, and Commerce*, the leading society of the Industrial Revolution, against which Blake railed by name in his notebooks.

Here, on the banks of the Thames, Los builded Golgonooza,
Outside the Gates of the Human Heart beneath Beulah
In the midst of the rocks of the Altars of Albion. In fears
He builded it, in rage & in fury. It is the Spiritual Fourfold
London, continually building & continually decaying desolate.
In eternal labours loud the Furnaces & loud the Anvils
Of Death thunder incessant.   684

This has now become the steady form of the cycle in which
man is always thwarted, and still must seek to fulfil himself:
'In immense labours & sorrows, ever building, ever falling'.

Blake faced the growth of industry resolutely. But its imagery
came to master and terrify his thought. It now shaped all his
symbolism: 'The Male is a Furnace of beryll, the Female is a
golden Loom'. It spoke in every passing likeness:

The key-bones & the chest dividing in pain
Disclose a hideous orifice; thence issuing, the Giant-brood
Arise, as the smoke of the furnace.   708

To feel this mounting horror, we should go from the genteel
tortures of Urizen by Los in *The Book of Urizen*, through those
of Fuzon by Urizen in *The Book of Ahania*, to the place in *Vala
or The Four Zoas* where the Females of Amalek enslave man,
singing:

O thou poor human form! O thou poor child of woe!
Why dost thou wander away from Tirzah? why me compell
  to bind thee?
If thou dost go away from me, I shall consume upon the
  rocks.
These fibres of thine eyes that used to wander in distant
  heavens
Away from me, I have bound down with a hot iron.
These nostrils that Expanded with delight in morning skies
I have bent downward with lead molten in my roaring
  furnaces.
My soul is seven furnaces, incessant roar the bellows
Upon my terribly flaming heart, the molten metal runs
In channels thro' my fiery limbs. O love! O pity! O pain!
O the pangs, the bitter pangs of love forsaken!

Ephraim was a wilderness of joy where all my wild beasts
ran.
The river Kanah wander'd by my sweet Manasseh's side.
Go, Noah, fetch the girdle of strong brass, heat it red hot,
Press it around the loins of this expanding cruelty.
Shriek not so, my only love.
Bind him down, sisters, bind him down on Ebal, mount of
cursing.
Malah, come forth from Lebanon, & Hoglah from Mount
Sinai,
Come circumscribe this tongue of sweets, & with a screw
of iron
Fasten this Ear into the Rock. Milcah, the task is thine.
Weep not so, sisters, weep not so; our life depends on this.   349

This is a spiritual crucifixion. But its horror comes from the
bodily world, and there was real. In the industrial parts of that
world, to which Blake gave symbols in *Jerusalem*—

Scotland pours out his Sons to labour at the Furnaces;
Wales gives his Daughters to the Looms   637

—the lives of fathers depended on such crucifixions.

FIVE

Blake had, of course, only a rough notion of the machines which
now stamped in his mind. He fills his mills with looms. In fact,
the mills were spinning-mills. Weaving was men's work, not
women's; and was taken into the factory only towards the end of
the time during which Blake was writing. And when Blake wrote
of the Surrey foundries, the larger ironmasters had long left that
and other charcoal scrubs, and were smelting with coke. Blake
knew how the factory had come to be called a mill. He recalled
the days of 'the water wheel & mill of many innumerable wheels
resistless', when it had looked like a mill. But he went on driving
the wheel by water, after the factory was changing to steam.
Blake's knowledge of the new world whose 'Work is Eternal Death
with Mills & Ovens & Cauldrons' is uncertain, because Blake had
it only from hearsay. There were some steam engines in London
breweries and waterworks throughout Blake's life. There were won-

ders like the Albion flour mill. But until Blake's last years industry
stayed out of London, in the North. He knew at first hand only
the brick kilns round London. Since Blake never went north of
London, he got his knowledge of the Derbyshire mills as he got
his knowledge of the Derbyshire countryside—

> from Mam-Tor to Dovedale,
> Discovering her own perfect beauty to the Daughters of
>   Albion: 726

he took both from others.

But although Blake's knowledge of industry was uncertain, his
vision of it was not. It is an astonishing vision. The reader must
turn the pages of the last prophetic books himself, at random:
and find everywhere the same sooty imagery, the air belched by
industry. Men of letters, whom the machine keeps clean, have
groped through this sulphurous rhetoric for the names tidily
listed in the books of mystics. The names are there, and they are
worth the finding. But Swedenborg the mystic had been an in-
spector of mines; Paine the deist planned iron bridges; Blake the
poet lived the Industrial Revolution bitterly, in the decay of his
engraver's craft. The oratory of *Vala or The Four Zoas*, of *Milton*,
and of *Jerusalem*, is loud with machines, with war, with law;
with the cry of man preying on man; and with the rebellious mutter
of working-men.

> Some fix'd the anvil, some the loom erected, some the plow
> And harrow form'd & fram'd the harness of silver & ivory,
> The golden compasses, the quadrant, & the rule & balance.
> They erected the furnaces, they form'd the anvils of gold
>   beaten in mills
> Where winter beats incessant, fixing them firm on their base.
> The bellows began to blow, & the Lions of Urizen stood round
>   the anvil
> And the leopards cover'd with skins of beasts tended the
>   roaring fires,
> [Sublime, distinct, their lineaments divine of human beauty.]
> The tygers of wrath called the horses of instruction from their
>   mangers,
> They unloos'd them & put on the harness of gold & silver &
>   ivory,
> In human forms distinct they stood round Urizen, prince of
>   Light,

Petrifying all the Human Imagination into rock & sand.
Groans ran along Tyburn's brook and along the River of
    Oxford
Among the Druid Temples. Albion groan'd on Tyburn's
    brook:
Albion gave his loud death groan. The Atlantic Mountains
    trembled.
Aloft the Moon fled with a cry: the Sun with streams of
    blood.
From Albion's Loins fled all Peoples and Nations of the Earth,
Fled with the noise of Slaughter, & the stars of heaven fled.
Jerusalem came down in a dire ruin over all the Earth,
She fell cold from Lambeth's Vales in groans & dewy
    death –
The dew of anxious souls, the death-sweat of the dying –
In every pillar'd hall & arched roof of Albion's skies.
The brother & the brother bathe in blood upon the Severn,
The Maiden weeping by. The father & the mother with
The Maiden's father & her mother fainting over the body,
And the Young Man, the Murderer, fleeing over the moun-
    tains.

281

In this world, the rebellious working-men broke machines. It
is not odd that, in this world, Blake turned his pitying and troubled
mind against the machine. To his mind, the machine became one
with the mechanics of Newton and the mechanical society of
Locke. The Satanic Wheels and the Satanic Mills are symbols for
the planetary orbits and the laws of gravitation which govern and
constrain them, filling 'the abstract Voids between the Stars' with
the machinery of Newton's astronomy. Blake saw in these laws
symbols, in their turn, of an abstract and inhuman society of con-
straint. Although these symbols are whimsical, what they say is
simple: that the machine was becoming master, in the theory
and in the practice of science—a giant orrery or planetarium 'to
turn that which is Soul & Life into a Mill or Machine'.

I turn my eyes to the Schools & Universities of Europe
And there behold the Loom of Locke, whose Woof rages
    dire,
Wash'd by the Water-wheels of Newton: black the cloth
In heavy wreathes folds over every Nation: cruel Works

> Of many Wheels I view, wheel without wheel, with cogs
>   tyrannic
> Moving by compulsion each other, not as those in Eden,
>   which,
> Wheel within Wheel, in freedom revolve in harmony &
>   peace.   636

These are the fancies of a puzzled man. Blake was blaming in
the machine the evil of which it is merely the tool. The tool was
so powerful that evil became a temptation which few could put
aside. But the evil remained the lust for profits, whatever the cost
to others; and that lust was older than the Industrial Revolution.
Owners and governments had grown stronger since then: they had
not changed otherwise. Blake wrote out the fear of the Yorkshire
croppers, and the nostalgia of craftsmen:

> Then left the Sons of Urizen the plow & harrow, the loom,
> The hammer & the chisel & the rule & compasses; from Lon-
>   don fleeing,
> They forg'd the sword on Cheviot, the chariot of war & the
>   battle-ax,
> The trumpet fitted to mortal battle, & the Flute of sum-
>   mer in Annandale;
> And all the Arts of Life they chang'd into the Arts of Death
>   in Albion.
> The hour-glass contemn'd because its simple workmanship
> Was like the workmanship of the plowman, & the water wheel
> That raises water into cisterns, broken & burn'd with fire
> Because its workmanship was like the workmanship of the
>   shepherd;
> And in their stead, intricate wheels invented, wheel without
>   wheel,
> To perplex youth in their outgoings & to bind to labours
>   in Albion
> Of day & night the myriads of eternity: that they may
>   grind
> And polish brass & iron hour after hour, laborious task,
> Kept ignorant of its use: that they might spend the days
>   of wisdom
> In sorrowful drudgery to obtain a scanty pittance of bread,
> In ignorance to view a small portion & think that All,
> And call it Demonstration, blind to all the simple rules of
>   life.   700

Plainly the argument of these lines will not hold. The machine does not grow evil because it grows more wheels than one—or because the wheels turn outside instead of inside one another, which was Blake's way of saying that the machine was moving away from the analogy of the human body. And Arkwright's mills had proved, from Mam-Tor to Dovedale, that the water-wheel can be used for evil no less than the steam engine. The enclosures had proved that the plough can murder as well as the chariot of war. Man is not freed from the profiteer because he is free of the mill. The society of the plough and the hand-loom shares the evil of our society: that men can be driven to do sorrowful drudgery, to obtain a scanty pittance of bread.

There were times when Blake thus granted his defeat. At such times he knew himself helpless before the actual, pitiful force of his own questioning. He saw the questions vividly. He saw the new harshness in the fight of owners against men, and the new violence done by the machines. He saw this at a time when there was only a handful of factories in England. And he set it down vividly. But beyond this, he could see only man's helplessness and his own. He could only pit good against evil, Los against Urizen, Orc against Los, in books of endless fight. He could only put off coming to an answer, in book after book of rhetoric and mystification. The answer got farther off, the prophetic books got longer. The censorship had got into Blake's mind: an uncertainty, what was left to say to a world whose puzzles had grown too hard and too bitter. At these times the prophetic books become pious but aimless rhetoric in the same meaning as the political nothings of Pitt, the quibbles of Wilberforce, and the mock rages of Burke. The Industrial Revolution had grown too large for them all.

SIX

Nevertheless, Blake was a more truthful man than these. He could not answer, but he did ask. He could not set right, but he knew the wrong. And even the fancies of the hour-glass against the chariot, of wheel within wheel against wheel without wheel, speak one truth. They mourn that the machine dominates the mind as well as the body, until it makes of the man at the machine another machine, stupid and at last beastly. They mourn the loss of a craft, for the craft's sake and for the sake of the men it made. 'A Machine is not a Man nor a Work of Art; it is destructive of Humanity & of Art; the word Machination.' Blake, whose own craft was dying as surely as the woolcomber's and the weaver's, was here writing in prophecy the story of his own life. 'Every honest man is a Prophet; he utters his opinion both of private & public matters. Thus: If you go on So, the result is So.'

In Blake's lifetime, his fame as a designer and engraver was at its greatest about the year 1796. In this year a bookseller asked Blake to make over five hundred coloured designs for Edward Young's *Night Thoughts*, which he would reprint with about two hundred engravings from these designs. Blake asked a hundred guineas for his designs. He was offered, and he had to take, twenty guineas. He was, of course, also paid for the work of engraving, at a higher price; although even this seems to have been less than the common rate. Yet when a first book with forty-three of these engravings was printed in 1797, there were no buyers for such spectacular folios. No other books were printed, and no bookseller would use Blake in such large plans again.

This story sums the decay of the craft to which Blake had served an apprenticeship of seven years. No machine had yet ousted the engraver. Daguerre did not invent his simple photography until 1839. But no new machine had yet ousted the frame-knitter; nevertheless, his livelihood was failing like Blake's. No doubt the folio of the *Night Thoughts* was killed by the money crisis of 1797. And the engraving of men whose manner was less personal than Blake's was not killed for many years. Engraving might have lasted Blake's lifetime; but it was doomed: and Blake's engraving died of the doom. He drifted to the patronage of Butts, and then to that of Hayley, which was more servile and became insufferable. He would have been wiser to stay in London and fight the bad years. For after Blake came back to London, in 1803, he never found more than hack-work which friends put his way. In 1805 he sold twelve designs for Robert Blair's *The Grave* for twenty guineas, in the hope of earning perhaps two hundred guineas for the engraving. When the book was printed, in 1808, the engraving had been done by another. After Joseph Johnson died in

1809, he fell to such work as engraving Flaxman's pottery designs for the Wedgwood catalogue. 'The Argument is better for Affluence than Poverty': William Blake, a sick man more than sixty years old, did his best work when John Linnell kept him after 1820.

And this is more than Blake's story. In this pattern, more violently, were failing the master workmen in every craft. Blake's father had paid fifty guineas in 1772 to apprentice him for seven years to the Basires, family craftsmen who remained engravers to the Society of Antiquaries for generations. But although Blake taught drawing and engraving, he never had an apprentice. Apprenticeship was dying in every craft. For apprenticeship is the safeguard of a society which has divided its work, but which still needs the whole of each man's output and skill. It belongs to an economy which is growing, but still stands in fear of famine. In fear of famine crafts are treasured: the craftsman must burden himself with the boy. And the boy, because his skill will be needed, has the whip hand of master and society. The apprentice of the Elizabethan plays is top dog.

But the economy of famine was past. The machines and the new farming were making their plenty. The apprentice no longer needed to be taught a skill. He became an unpaid child worker, against whose use Spitalfields weavers and Nottingham knitters rioted throughout the eighteenth century. Henry Carey's verses show that he had lost the whip hand before 1720.

> When she is by I leave my Work,
>   (I love her so sincerely)
> My Master comes like any Turk,
>   And bangs me most severely;
> But, let him bang his Belly-full,
>   I'll bear it all for *Sally*;
> She is the Darling of my Heart,
>   And she lives in our Alley.

Throughout the eighteenth century, magistrates had their courts full of the complaints of apprentices. Their masters had taken them only for the binding money, could teach them no craft but to steal, and were banging them most severely, merely to drive them away. In 1747 a shipwright sued his apprentice, who had run away to sea, for £1,200 prize money which the boy had won there. His right to the boy's earnings could not be denied in law. At the end of the century parish children were being carted to the mills from as far as London, to be apprentices in name. They were pitilessly turned out of the mills whenever a slump closed them.

The economy of famine was past. Plenty had come to the mill and the farm. But it had not come to the mill-hand and the farm-hand. They still worked, they still work, as if they had desperately to stave off famine. Just before he began *Vala or The Four Zoas*, Blake had written some simple verses for *The Song of Los*, from which he quoted in later books. With the precise and delicate movement which was now failing his prophetic books, he there spoke his mind and his heart together.

> Shall not the King call for Famine from the heath,
> Nor the Priest for Pestilence from the fen,
> To restrain, to dismay, to thin
> The inhabitants of mountain and plain,
> In the day of full-feeding prosperity
> And the night of delicious songs?
>   Shall not the Councellor throw his curb
> Of Poverty on the laborious,
> To fix the price of labour,
> To invent allegoric riches?
>   And the privy admonishers of men
> Call for fires in the City,
> For heaps of smoking ruins
> In the night of prosperity & wantonness?
>   To turn man from his path,
> To restrain the child from the womb,
> To cut off the bread from the city,
> That the remnant may learn to obey,
>   That the pride of the heart may fail,
> That the lust of the eyes may be quench'd,
> That the delicate ear in its infancy
> May be dull'd, and the nostrils clos'd up,
> To teach mortal worms the path
> That leads from the gates of the Grave? 247

There is an age of history in these lines. There is the history of the struggle of the eighteenth-century workmen to free the price

of labour, which the Elizabethan Statute of Artificers still con-
trolled. Fox and Whitbread were pressing for a Minimum Wages
Bill, in the very year 1795 when this was etched. There is Blake's
understanding that, in the inflation of the French wars, a minimum
wage would yield only allegoric riches. There may be a hint of
other allegoric riches, in another world, which Wesley and Whitefield had promised the miners. There is the history of the planned
riot in Birmingham in 1791. There may be a hint of the City-
planned Gordon riots. But deeper than all history is the contrast,
that Church and King call for plague and famine,

> To restrain, to dismay, to thin
> The inhabitants of mountain and plain,
> In the day of full-feeding prosperity.   247

Prosperity for masters, famine for men: Blake has suddenly looked
past King and Priest, past Councellor and *agent provocateur*, to
the contradiction at the heart of his society—

> Heaps of smoking ruins
> In the night of prosperity & wantonness.   247

Years later, England was suffering the great slump which followed the peace of 1815. Then, one thoughtful Whig wrote to
another:

> I dare not trust myself to speak of politics, my sentiments are
> so very different from those which are popular. It appears
> that there are one or two problems in political economy which
> have never been solved by any writer from Smith to Dumont.
>   Why has the return of peace plunged every part of the
> British Empire into pecuniary distress?
>   How has plenty produced poverty?

The thought, and the words, were new even then. But Blake
had seen the man-made famine in the plenty, more than twenty
years before. He had understood the two economies between which
his livelihood had failed. His apprenticeship had looked back to
the economy of famine, which had paid a wage only to those who
made a full share of its needs. And his working life was unmanned
by the economy of profits, made that a few men might take more
than a share of an industrial society's glut. He had seen his so-

ciety torn by these contraries, yet driven only by the tension between them; and he had seen this in 1795. Blake did not share Humphry Davy's assurance, that only by this tension could industry live. All his life he hated these 'sources of power in civilized life', and believed, all his life, that 'Poverty is the Fool's Rod'. This is the Last Judgement which he sought, in the body and in the spirit: to make a nobler progression from the contraries of famine and plenty.

SEVEN

And it is not chance that Blake chose these words himself.

> Without Contraries is no progression. Attraction and Repulsion, Reason and Energy, Love and Hate, are necessary to Human existence.
>
> From these contraries spring what the religious call Good & Evil. Good is the passive that obeys Reason. Evil is the active springing from Energy.
>
> Good is Heaven. Evil is Hell. 149

The words come from *The Marriage of Heaven and Hell*, etched about 1790. The book is named to show the progression of its contraries, and of Swedenborg's. And it shows that Blake made for himself, twenty years before Hegel, the dialectic of Hegel's formal thought. Blake took his contraries from his industrial society, above all from the double dealing which he read in its religion. To the end of his life, he was fascinated by the symbol of the hypocrite: 'At the same time I cannot well reconcile it with the will of God'. He saw in the progression, always renewed, the strife of 'the Holy Ghost, who in Paine strives with Christendom as in Christ he strove with the Jews'. His social thought spoke in religious dislikes. But it did not miss in the priest the outlook of the master, 'the passive that obeys Reason'. Blake hated that thought, in the mechanical action and reaction of Newton, and in the mechanical society of Newton's friend Locke. Their merchant age was over. The new industry could be righted only in a progression of their contraries. He saw it fail in the famine mechanism of mere negation, in body and in spirit, knowing that—

> Negations are not Contraries: Contraries mutually Exist;
> But Negations Exist Not.   639

It is not chance that the most searching study of the war of
society with itself was begun, seventy-five years after Blake, by
Karl Marx from the same dialectic.

This at last is the crux of Blake's thought. The vagueness of
the prophetic books, their shifting rhetoric, their helpless long-
windedness: the censorship of an age, and the censorship in
Blake's mind: these do not make them hard to understand. They
merely make them hard to read without letting the mind wander.
But there is a twofoldness in them and, twofold within twofold,
a manifoldness, which are hard. The gods break and fight, the
symbols shift and divide, in bewildering contraries. Los the light
fights against Urizen, and at once Orc the fire fights against Los.
Los and Enitharmon, symbols of the age of iron and textiles, are
also male and female, spectre and emanation: 'But my Emanation,
Alas! will become My Contrary': are a whole, yet each itself divided.
The division of contraries, and their progression to Blake's single
thought, are the bases of his thought. It is not a trifling thought.
That is why Blake's many Prometheus symbols, Los, Fuzon, Orc,
have none of the childishness of Shelley's Prometheus. Industry
is not a single hope and blessing to them, as it is to Prometheus.
They are at odds within themselves, masters and men, Reason,
and Energy by turns, at every turn. Blake did not share Shelley's
faith in the reach-me-down Utopia of William Godwin—

> The chains fall off of themselves, when the magic of opinion
> is dissolved.

He strove for the progression of man from his society, to be man
himself. This progression goes from the prophetic books to the
poems. The prophetic books stand against the evil of Blake's society. But the poems stand against the evil wish of man—'with
a screw of iron Fasten this Ear into the Rock'—

> That the pride of the heart may fail,
> That the lust of the eyes may be quench'd
> That the delicate ear in its infancy
> May be dull'd, and the nostrils clos'd up,
> To teach mortal worms the path
> That leads from the gates of the Grave.   247

For Blake did not shirk this last step: beyond how man is to
live, to what man is to be. That is why the states of man symbolized in his cities are not threefold but fourfold. The threefold is society, its energetic contrary, and their progression to a new
society. But this new society is itself only the first of a new threefold, in the same cycle. This progression makes an endless set of
social threefolds. There is an end to this for Blake, not in societies,
but in man. There the threefold reaches the fourth state, Jerusalem.
The social urges had the religious force of an ideal for Blake.
We should be wanting in reading if we missed the social urges.
But we should be wanting in honesty if we let them close our
minds to his ideal. It is our pride that Blake proved, in himself,
that a mind given to the spirit can share our anger at the hardships with which a society thwarts its men. We should wrong that
pride in bigotry if we praised the anger and belittled the spirit.
For Blake's was an anger of the spirit, which felt the hardships of
his fellows working with their hands, not as suffering and not
as waste, but as a wrong. The end which he sought was more
than a social righting: it was the right. He believed that this
end is found in no society, but must be found by man himself.
We owe it to him to follow to the end, from the public speech
of the prophetic books, into the self of his poems.

INNOCENCE AND EXPERIENCE

Dissent

ONE

No symbol in Blake is single and fixed: for Blake looks at none in a fixed way.

> A fourfold vision is given to me;
> 'Tis fourfold in my supreme delight
> And threefold in soft Beulah's night
> And twofold Always. May God us keep
> From Single vision & Newton's sleep!   818

Even Newton is not always the single symbol of a narrow rationalism which he is here. He is also the energetic spirit with the compasses in Blake's colour print of *Newton*, and the spirit who blows the trump of the Last Judgement in *Europe*. His are the compasses with which Urizen marks out the Mundane Shell in the greatest of Blake's designs, which is commonly named *The Ancient of Days*. They are also the compasses of the child Jesus in Blake's design of *Christ in the Carpenter's Shop*. This shift, from one arm to the other, of the Freemason compasses of rationalism, is part of the movement of the Industrial Revolution. And it is Blake's movement between innocence and experience.

The god whom Blake destroys again in each prophetic book is the bible Jehovah, Urizen. Yet he is a symbol moved to evil less by will than by compulsion. His changes in *The Book of Urizen* are also the changes of man in Blake's poem *The Mental Traveller*. The harshest of these changes is that which, in one engraving to *The Book of Urizen*, sinks him *In the Waters of*

135

Materialism. There Urizen forgets that the mind is whole, and sinks to mere reasoning. Blake did not forget.

> Reason, or the ratio of all we have already known, is not the same that it shall be when we know more.   97
> He who sees the Infinite in all things, sees God. He who sees the Ratio only, sees himself only.   98
> Reason is the bound or outward circumference of Energy.   149
> The bounded is loathed by its possessor. The same dull round, even of a universe, would soon become a mill with complicated wheels.   97

Reasoning, the mill, and the machine worlds of Newton and of Locke are already parts of one symbol about 1788, when Blake etched five of these six sentences. Six years later, the symbol had become Urizen, and had become, in Blake's dialectic, the contrary of innocence. Therefore, *The Book of Urizen* moves straight into *The Book of Ahania*, where Urizen is mastered by Fuzon. The contraries of Your Reason and Innocence have their progression in Fusion.

Nevertheless, Blake did not belittle Urizen in his design *The Ancient of Days*, which he put on the first page of *Europe*. He coloured a print of the design lovingly on his death-bed. Blake knew that the Mundane Shell must be marked out and made.

> Terrific Urizen strode above in fear & pale dismay.
> He saw the indefinite space beneath & his soul shrunk with horror;
> His feet upon the verge of Non Existence; his voice went forth:
> > Luvah & Vala trembling & shrinking beheld the great Work master
> And heard his Word: 'Divide, ye bands, influence by influence.
> Build we a Bower for heaven's darling in the grizzly deep:
> [Build we the Mundane Shell around the Rock of Albion.']
> > The Bands of Heaven flew thro' the air singing & shouting to Urizen.
> Some fix'd the anvil, some the loom erected, some the plow
> And harrow form'd & fram'd the harness of silver & ivory,
> The golden compasses, the quadrant, & the rule & balance.   280

As the building goes on, the contraries needs come to battle: 'Divide, ye bands, influence by influence.' Yet Blake knew that this twofoldness is the price which Existence pays, not to be Non-existence. He attacks Urizen, precisely for bounding the contraries with law and with religion: 'One Law for the Lion & Ox is Oppression.' The 'Single vision & Newton's sleep' are at fault, because they cripple the progression from these contraries of innocence and experience. In seeing this, Blake looked searchingly into the abuses of rationalism.

TWO

Isaac Newton's *Philosophiae Naturalis Principia Mathematica* had been printed in 1687, at the beginning of the Whig age. Richard Bentley, greatest of Whig scholars and bullies, had at once made 'the Eternal Laws of Gravitation' another name for Nature. And Whig society, happy to learn that nature was so ordered, honoured Newton justly. But the honour was not paid to science: it was paid to order. Bentley was not a scientist, but a divine anxious to prove the world held in a god-given order. John Ray and others put their science to the same use. Bentley had Newton's blessing in founding his order on gravitation. He chose gravitation, because he rightly saw that it closed post-Renaissance astronomy. Throughout the Whig age, Newton's and other sciences were not tools for fresh discovery. They were used to close and enclose the world in another system as rigid as that of Aristotle, which the medieval church had put to the same use. It was an age of systematizers, who sought in science the assurance that the world could be tidied away inside the head of a rational Whig god. This is why Blake held that its atomism was 'to Educate a Fool how to build a Universe with Farthing Balls'.

For Blake disliked the heritage of these systems, not alone because they were rigid, but because they were abstract. It may seem odd that he should have coupled Newton's world of compulsion with the indefinite manner of engraving which he hated. He saw in both the same threat, that the actual would be lost in the manner or the system. He saw the thing pictured dissolve in 'dots & lozenges', 'unorganized Blots & Blurs'. And he saw the actual thing dissolve in the law of nature, where matter becomes mere 'globes of attraction'. But 'Identities or Things are Neither Cause nor Effect. They are Eternal.' Therefore Newton's system was to him at once fixed and indefinite. Blake followed Berkeley in finding a target for both dislikes in Newton's fluxions, that is his method of infinitesimals.

> I know too well that a great majority of Englishmen are fond of The Indefinite which they Measure by Newton's Doctrine of the Fluxions of an Atom, A Thing that does not Exist. These are Politicians & think that Republican Art is Inimical to their Atom. For a Line or Lineament is not formed by Chance: a Line is a Line in its Minutest Subdivisions: Strait or Crooked It is Itself & Not Intermeasurable with or by any Thing Else. Such is Job, but since the French Revolution Englishmen are all Intermeasurable One by Another, Certainly a happy state of Agreement to which I for One do not Agree.   878

To Blake, the thing must remain itself, in its most 'Minute Particulars'; and is itself, because these are its particulars alone. In Newton's open and infinite space the thing was held to its form by gravitational forces, and the universe held together only by such forces. Blake sought to construct a universe of a piece, which held together, in the large and in the small, of itself. In place of mechanics, such a construct must have a geometry of its own. Blake worked out this geometry.

> The nature of infinity is this: That every thing has its
> Own Vortex, and when once a traveller thro' Eternity
> Has pass'd that Vortex, he percieves it roll backward behind
> His path, into a globe itself infolding.   497

> The Vegetative Universe opens like a flower from the Earth's center
> In which is Eternity. It expands in Stars to the Mundane Shell
> And there it meets Eternity again, both within and without.   633

This is a remarkable construct for Blake to have pictured. For it cannot be put into a space of only three dimensions. And Blake knew this.

The Mundane Shell is a vast Concave Earth, an immense
Harden'd shadow of all things upon our Vegetated Earth,
Enlarg'd into dimension & deform'd into indefinite space.   498

Since Blake made his picture by analogy, we cannot be sure
what his universe was. If he drew the analogy from a flat world,
his construct is a solid which is an analogue of the surface of a
ring. If he drew it from a spherical world, his construct is the
solid which is the analogue of the surface of a sphere. Either solid
is strikingly such a universe as Blake sought: for both are finite,
but have no bounding surfaces. Against this, Blake saw in Newton's
universe the worst of abstractions, at once infinite and constrained.
This is a biased view of Newton's great system, but it is not a
false view. On the same view, Blake found the painting, the
thought, and the society of his time arbitrary and indefinite together. In his symbol, each was 'A dark black Rock & a gloomy
Cave'; and each was Newton. Blake's was an imagination of pictures, astonishing in its geometrical insight. And he was a man
who all his life worked with his hands: who wanted a world to
hold together of itself, having a self to hold.

THREE

It has been argued that Newton also made his world as a craftsman, to meet the needs of his time. Certainly post-Renaissance
astronomy grew from questions asked by navigators. And the
needs of navigators were still pressing in the trading age of Newton.
But the needs were no longer for answers: they were for tools.
The large questions of navigation had been answered before
Newton was born. For example, it was known how to find latitude
with the quadrant and longitude with the clock. What was not
known was how to make a good quadrant, and a clock which
would keep time at sea. Newton knew of these needs. He sketched
a quadrant which, had he made it, might have saved others thirty
years of work. But he did not make it. His great work could
answer questions recondite as those of the tides. It did nothing to
meet the pressing needs of a society of merchant sailors who still
could not tell where they were at sea. Their needs were met by

craftsmen such as John Harrison, who made a clock to go at sea, but found it hard to get the prize money which the Government had offered for it. A hundred years before Blake, the Royal Society had been founded for such workman-like ends. It had begun in this English tradition, in the experiments of Robert Boyle, in the statistics of William Petty, and in the quick invention of Robert Hooke. But the twenty-five years of Newton's presidency from 1703 put aside this tradition, and designedly killed much that its great handymen had begun. For fifty years before Blake was born, science was a belittled craft for workmen. The Royal Society became a club, first for systematizers, and then for elderly lords. In 1754 the ends which it had once set itself had to be set afresh by a self-taught mechanic, for the *Society for the Encouragement of Arts, Manufactures, and Commerce*. Men so learned as Samuel Johnson still believed that swallows winter underwater. Laurence Sterne's *Tristram Shandy* mocked one of the most useful steps then taken by medicine, Dr Burton's forceps. The experimenter was an untidy oddity in a world which such men were glad to have science prove orderly, but not to change. Their classical learning, which Blake's notes to Dr Thornton's *New Translation of the Lord's Prayer* attacked bitterly, did not reach its *reductio ad absurdum* until 1805. In that year Lord Eldon, richest, most grasping, and most bigoted of Chief Justices, laid it down in law that an endowed Grammar School may not teach mathematics and modern languages.

While these men entrenched themselves in the rationalism of *let be*, the Industrial Revolution was being made by more energetic minds. Hargreaves, Highs, Crompton; the Darbys and the Wilkinsons; Newcomen, Watt, and Trevithick; Rennie and other builders of canals, lighthouses, bridges, and roads: these were not men who showed scientific toys at the Royal Society. They were men who had learnt what they knew with their hands, in order to make their hands work better: at the loom, the furnace, the mine, and the lathe. Their active rationalism also would end in sand: Blake saw it do so before he died; but now it lived and created. To simpler men of their stamp, the *Society for the Encouragement of Arts, Manufactures, and Commerce* gave its prizes: for good paper and varnish, good butter and saltpetre; for growing swedes and forests; for new tools, new dyes, new ways of sowing, of weaving, of sweeping chimneys. The Society gave prizes to sculptors whom Blake knew, among them Flaxman and John Bacon. The growth of industry indeed soon made its knowledge belated, so that it tended to shrink as its name has shrunk in speech, to the *Society of Arts*. But even its show of drawings, which made one beginning for the Royal Academy, had been prompted by the needs of industrial draughtsmanship. It is in this lively tradition that Blake put into the hands of Urizen, of the young Newton, and of Jesus the child carpenter, 'the golden compasses, the quadrant, & the rule & balance'. Blake was seeing them as craftsmen with a new tool, as Benjamin Franklin had just seen man anew as a tool-making animal. Urizen is here one with the great makers of clocks and precision instruments, Graham, Bird, Dollond, Ramsden, in whose workshops, already models of the division of labour, young mechanics such as Watt learned their craft. These were such men as Huntsman, who, to make a better watch-spring, spent a lifetime in making the best steel which has been made. When Arkwright took out his first patent for the spinning-frame, he posed as a clockmaker, that is a precision mechanic. For as Arkwright's counsel said when the patent was attacked and overthrown in 1785, by a combination of manufacturers guided by Peel,

> It is well known that the most useful discoveries that have been made in every branch of art and manufactures have not been made by speculative philosophers in their closets, but by ingenious mechanics, conversant in the practices in use in their time, and practically acquainted with the subject-matter of their discoveries.

FOUR

In the nineteenth century these men came to crowd the mechanics' institutes. The institutes had their forerunners in the manufacturing towns of the Industrial Revolution, in the Midlands and in the North. John Dalton, a weaver's son, became a great chemist in the Manchester Literary and Philosophical Society. Generations of working men learned biology from the nice doggerel of Erasmus

Darwin, grandfather of Charles Darwin, and a founder of the Lunar Society of Birmingham between 1766 and 1775.

The men in these societies were commonly owners who had grown up in their industries, and had made them. Such men were Boulton, Watt, perhaps Wilkinson, and others of the Lunar Society. John Roebuck, who by then had settled in Scotland, and James Keir were pioneers of the Midland chemical industry. Josiah Wedgwood had found how to measure high temperatures in his pottery, and for it. William Small linked these men with other scientists, among them those of America, where he had been professor of mathematics. He helped to find for Watt's engine the workmanship of Boulton and of Wilkinson. And Joseph Priestley, son of a Yorkshire cropper and brother-in-law of Wilkinson, showed that a non-industrial scientist could share the robust gifts of his fellows in the Lunar Society. When Priestley studied electricity, he invented electrotyping. When he studied carbon dioxide, he made soda water, and the Admiralty hoped that it might cure scurvy. When he made oxygen, he thought of its use against diseases of the lungs. He left it to others to found a new system of chemistry on his knowledge of oxygen. And Priestley began his researches from a practical knack: he found how to collect gases, over water or mercury.

Such men were making more than the skeleton of the world which we know: lighthouses and engines, roads and iron bridges, gas and electricity, chemicals and farming. They were doing more than helping to end drugging and bleeding, and to spread the knowledge of a natural medicine: anatomy, inoculation, chest tapping, the thermometer; simples like digitalis and castor oil; the cleanliness of the cotton dress and of the iron bed. They ended the magical faith in tar water, which Berkeley had shared; and the belief of the doctors of the 1720s that Mary Tofts of Godalming had given birth to rabbits. For lack of such men, half Europe has remained not merely a backward but a dark continent.

These men did not close their rationalism in the private worlds of Berkeley, the anti-causality of Hume, and the formalism of the Physiocrat economists: all the thought then fleeing gracefully to weep into urns in country vicarages. They were not content to think that, because the world is rational, it is fixed; and that, be-

cause there are laws of nature, every law is given by nature. That
Whig rationalism had

> wept, & built
> Tombs in the desolate places,
> And form'd laws of prudence, and call'd them
> The eternal laws of God.   236

But to these lively and questioning dissenters, rationalism was
not the end but the beginning of thought. If the world is rational,
then the results of action can be foreseen and tested. Therefore
their rationalism urged them to act. It prompted them to question the nature in the laws, and made, step by step, Voltaire's
Candide, Rousseau's *Contrat Social*, the Declaration of Independence, and the *Rights of Man* of the French Revolution and of
Tom Paine. It read Berkeley as a materialist and Hume as an
atheist; and turned the Physiocrat diagram into the historical
thought of Adam Smith. Just so Newton's astronomy was taken no
farther in England, but became a new science in the France of
the *Encyclopédie*, in Blake's youth; for there it was held not to
prove but to challenge the hand of God. Only when this dissenting
rationalism in turn was wrested to evil, in the defeat of the French
Revolution and in the mastery of the machine, did Blake cast it
out as one with Newton's. Then he laid aside the symbol of the
compasses, and heard only the inhuman roll of the wheel. Urizen
at the head of *Europe* in 1794 had still been the Great Work
Master, a monument to the dignity of labour, thinking by doing.

FIVE

Blake belonged to the dissenting masters and men, by trade, by
stock, and by tradition—a hidden Puritan tradition that ran back,
in language and radical belief, to the Levellers and the Diggers.
Although more mystical than Priestley, he shared the same Christian zeal. Priestley had written his *History of the Corruptions of
Christianity* to attack 'what has so long passed for Christianity'.
So Blake held that only 'the Perversions of Christ's words & acts are
attack'd by Paine'; and so, at the age of sixty, he still wrote against
the common view:

Was Jesus Humble? or did he
Give any Proofs of Humility?
Boast of high Things with Humble tone,
And give with Charity a Stone?   751

He scorn'd Earth's Parents, scorn'd Earth's God,
And mock'd the one & the other's Rod;
His Seventy Disciples sent
Against Religion & Government.   757

This was the tradition, and this was the stock, which made the
Industrial Revolution. The mining engineers, the textile inventors, the potters, the instrument makers, the ironmasters were
nearly all dissenters. Graham, the Darbys, Huntsman, Dalton, and
others were Quakers. Samuel Crompton was a follower of Swedenborg. A hundred years before Blake, William Petty had foreseen
this, in the form in which R. H. Tawney has shown it since:
that these were the vigorous, workman-like, sober, and saving men,
self-taught and with a tradition of thinking for themselves.
Most of Blake's fellow artists were dissenters; and Blake wrote,
'The unproductive Man is not a Christian'. The dissenting
academies were the best scientific schools of the century, and
stood above the Universities. Here Priestley, Richard Price, Gilbert Wakefield, and others learned and taught. The learned societies drew their strength from these academies, above all the
Manchester Literary and Philosophical Society from Warrington
Academy. The dissenting tradition proved its firmness of thought
in the American war, and held it beyond the French Revolution.
The Friendly Societies and the craft unions of dissenting workmen
made the core of the Corresponding Societies. The secret report on
the West Country food riots in the famine year of 1801 holds that
the rioters

were certainly directed by inferior Tradesmen, Wool-combers
and Dissenters, who keep aloof, but by their language and
immediate influence, govern the lower classes.

The numerous association of Wool-combers (who as they
boast consist of sixty thousand persons in different parts of the
Kingdom) being for the most part Dissenters are the just
objects of attention to Government, and to those who support

the constitution of Great Britain against Republican machinations.

SIX

Against this strain of Unitarian dissent, another strain had grown powerful from the time of Blake's birth. This was the evangelical strain of Wesley and Whitefield. Both men had first preached in 1739 to the colliers of Kingswood near Bristol, then stirring with the discontent which broke out in the great food riots of miners in 1740. Although their message of mystical submission moved the rich as well as the poor, it was always most apt to those who worked without hope.

> The Countess of Huntingdon was also anxious that the colliers on the Tyne should share the blessing which the colliers of Kingswood had already found.

At this time miners in Scotland were still serfs in law, bound to the mine for life: Parliament passed Acts to free them in 1775 and 1799. The fervour of the miners of the Industrial Revolution for the mysticism of Wesley has a striking likeness to the fervour with which the slave miners of Greece and her colonies had taken up the mysticism of Pythagoras, more than two thousand years before. Blake saw the mysticism and the chapel fervour starkly.

> They reduce the Man to want, then give with pomp & ceremony:
> The praise of Jehovah is chaunted from lips of hunger &
> thirst.   656

John Wesley was an outspoken Tory. The selfless salvation in the will of God which he preached was coupled, in his tracts, with a selfless submission in the laws of man. He renewed such societies as the *Society for the Reformation of Manners*, which Defoe had once left in anger because it spied on no vices but those of the poor. These were the societies which, towards the end of Blake's life, made it their task to trap those who sold the books of Paine and Shelley. In 1792 the Wesleyan statutes laid it down that

L

> None of us shall either in writing or in conversation speak lightly or irreverently of the Government. We are to observe that the oracles of God command us to be subject to the higher powers; and that honour to the King is there connected with the fear of God.

The Wesleyan manifesto of 1811 could claim justly that evangelical dissent had been powerful, for more than fifty years,

> in raising the standard of public morals, and in promoting loyalty in the middle ranks, as well as subordination and industry in the lower orders of society.

The need for these virtues was urgent at the time. The Luddite riots began in this year. When later the magistrates rounding up Luddites took by mistake a Wesleyan preacher, a Wesleyan philanthropist put the need to them plainly:

> I have had ample information that the lower orders who are not religiously inclined are in a very disaffected, discontented state, and are almost ripe for a general revolt.

Blake did not share the submission in a god-given society which Methodism was hardening in the phrase, 'the lower orders'. And there were Methodist doctrines whose infection he dreaded, 'the infection of Sin & stern Repentance'. Nevertheless, Blake felt the movement from rationalist to evangelical dissent. The beginnings of this movement had been away from the deist divinity of works, to the divinity of grace by faith alone. Wesley later checked this; but the debate remained vivid to Blake, restless between these contraries of experience and innocence. In the days of the Paine set, in 1788, he had stressed the working rationalism of experience.

> As the true method of knowledge is experiment, the true faculty of knowing must be the faculty which experiences. This faculty I treat of. 98

But as he saw his hopes fail and turn to evil, he came to stress inspiration as the greater good. And in time, he moved farther, almost to orthodox divinity. The call *To the Deists in Jerusalem* unsays a lifetime of hope.

You, O Deists, profess yourselves the Enemies of Christianity, and you are so: you are also the Enemies of the Human Race & of Universal Nature. Man is born a Spectre or Satan & is altogether an Evil, & requires a New Selfhood continually, & must continually be changed into his direct Contrary. But your Greek Philosophy (which is a remnant of Druidism) teaches that Man is Righteous in his Vegetated Spectre: an Opinion of fatal & accursed consequence to Man, as the Ancients saw plainly by Revelation, to the intire abrogation of Experimental Theory.   682

This would be a formal setting out of Original Sin and of grace, were it not brought to life by the belief which is Blake's own, in the endless renewal of contraries in progression. This holds together Wesley's dissent and Priestley's, innocence to experience. And Blake did hold them together, in a wish which both traditions of dissent had in common. The wish was, to make a whole man who should remain a child.

SEVEN

The poets of the turn of that century, Blake, Wordsworth, Coleridge, and Shelley, shared this cult of the child. The cult had many scattered beginnings, which have in common a growing dislike of social man. Mandeville and Swift had disliked his savagery, and had fabled of societies of animals with a more rational self-interest. Rousseau had disliked his self-interest, and had fabled of a nobler society of savagery. The dislike was now being turned against towns and against industry, in which children played their pitiful part. There are hints of all these beginnings in the writings of humanitarian dissenters, such as Blake and Coleridge were. To them, the child became a twofold Christian symbol: innocence, the symbol of pity; and experience, Christ the child teacher become a teacher of children.

The first symbol is uppermost in the minds of those humanitarians who tried to check the dying of parish children. They had begun the Foundling Hospital in 1739, and had won Hanway's Act to board out these children in 1767. The carting of children to the mills at the end of the century, and the battles over their working hours which followed, show how hard was the task of humanitarians. They fought against interests which did not yield until they had little to lose. And where the interests were few, humanitarians fought against endless indifference. One story will tell how long they might fight. Since 1767, Hanway had been trying to free the apprentices to chimney sweepers from their dangerous and cancerous work. Societies such as the *Society for Ameliorating the Condition of Infant Chimney-Sweepers* had been formed since 1773. A paper Act had been passed on behalf of these boys in 1788. And when Blake wrote his two poems *The Chimney Sweeper*, before 1794, prizes were being offered for sweeping machines. Yet in 1824 Charles Lamb was still sending one of Blake's poems to the Quaker poet Barton, for James Montgomery's *Chimney-Sweeper's Friend and Climbing Boy's Album*. Lamb added frankly:

> Montgomery's book I have not much hope from. The Society, with the affected name, has been labouring at it for these 20 years, and made few converts.

The Lords were not among the converts: they threw out four Bills on behalf of the climbing boys in the 1820s. The boys did not begin to be set free until 1834. Blake alone was more forgotten. When Lamb wrote, he did not know that Blake was alive.

The symbol of Christ the teacher of children was not less urgent. At the beginning of the Whig age, Locke had laid it down that, 'Knowledge and science in general are the business only of those who are at ease and leisure.' Mandeville had pointed the meaning of this plainly:

> Men who are to remain and end their days in a Laborious, Tiresome and Painful Station of Life, the sooner they are put upon it at first, the more patiently they'll submit to it for ever after.

Dissenting workmen saw as plainly that their children could therefore rise from their station, only if they were taught above it. Therefore their Sunday schools taught children at least to read, even before Blake was born. Other dissenting schools tried to teach them more. The Foundling Hospital had been planned to teach

:hildren no more than their trade. But in 1799 it had to grant hat

> Different occupations and manufactures for the boys have been at times introduced into the Hospital. The last that has been tried with much effect and continuance has been the spinning of worsted yarn. It was however attended with this inconvenience, that the boys who had been so employed were not so much in request as apprentices, and were not placed out so speedily or so well as those whose writing, reading and accounts had been more attended to.

Nevertheless, when Samuel Whitbread in 1807 brought in a bill to have all children taught, he was answered as Locke and as Mandeville had answered. The patron of science Giddy, later president of the Royal Society, was disarming:

> However specious in theory the project might be, of giving education to the labouring classes of the poor, it would in effect be found to be prejudicial to their morals and happiness; it would teach them to despise their lot in life, instead of making them good servants in agriculture, and other laborious employments to which their rank in society had destined them; instead of teaching them subordination, it would render them factious and refractory, as was evident in the manufacturing counties; it would enable them to read seditious pamphlets, vicious books, and publications against Christianity; it would render them insolent to their superiors; and in a few years the result would be that the legislature would find it necessary to direct the strong arm of power towards them, and to furnish the executive magistrate with much more vigorous laws than were now in force.

So said Lord Eldon; so said the Archbishop of Canterbury. The Lords threw out the bill.

This downright view was not shared by evangelical dissenters. They did not care to take teaching far: they made the Sunday schools pious, and killed the dissenting academies. But they believed that Christian books could help to strengthen and content the poor. And unlike the Lords, they did not think that their books need be less readable than the publications against Christianity. Certainly the writings of Wesley, of Wilberforce, and of the Religious Tract Society of Hannah More were widely read. But the most readable evangelical books were written for children. Isaac Watts, in his *Divine Songs, for the use of Children*, had begun this purposeful tradition in 1715, when Wesley himself was still a child.

> In Works of Labour or of Skill
>   I would be busy too:
> For *Satan* finds some Mischief still
>   For idle Hands to do.
>
> In Books, or Work, or healthful Play,
>   Let my first Years be past,
> That I may give for every Day
>   Some good Account at last.

Watts had written of his book as 'a slight specimen, such as I could wish some happy and condescending genius would undertake for the use of children, and perform much better'. It has been pointed out by others that Blake may have been prompted by this wish, when he wrote his *Songs of Innocence*. Certainly Blake began his book as a book for children, with a knowledge of other books for children. The bookseller John Newbery had set a fashion for such books, just before Blake was born: it is said that Oliver Goldsmith wrote *Goody Two Shoes* for him. Blake himself designed and engraved the plates for a book for children by Mary Wollstonecraft, *Original Stories, From Real Life*, which Joseph Johnson printed. And Blake first engraved his *Gates of Paradise* as a picture book of the kind which Newbery had sold widely, to teach children to read.

Rationalist and evangelical dissent shared this tradition; and both enriched Blake's poems. But so gifted and liberal a rationalist as the banker William Roscoe, who wished to renew the Italy of Lorenzo the Magnificent in Liverpool, could not make his books for children more than fanciful. Blake in his poems found a simpler speech which is more searching, and an imagery more moving and more vivid: the easy speech and the mighty imagery of the Methodist revival.

Innocence and Experience

When Blake was born, the eighteenth-century manner was dying. Even in the sensuous hands of Pope, alive in *The Rape of the Lock* to each shade of colour, of sound, and of touch, the manner had lacked imagery. It had taken its life from Pope's breathless ear and ruthless clarity. When these were lost, nothing was left to mark two lines of Gray,

> Fair Science frown'd not on his humble birth,
> And Melancholy mark'd him for her own,

from two lines of John Freeth, the Political Songster of Birmingham,

> Blest Navigation! source of golden days
> Which Commerce finds, and brightens all its ways.

Both men are thinking elevated clap-trap; and, since they think without imagery, both are writing doggerel.

Gray tried to give life to his writing in 1757 in his *Odes*, by adding to this an imagery of violence. Burke had just urged such imagery, in his *Philosophical Inquiry into the Origin of our Ideas of the Sublime and the Beautiful*. And it had been used fifteen years before, in the two poems for which Blake was later thought most fitted to design: the *Night Thoughts* of Edward Young and *The Grave* of Robert Blair. Unhappily, the decay of the eighteenth-century manner lay deeper than in tricks of speech. The gloom and the indecision of the *Elegy Written in a Country Church-*

yard had been those of a dying society. They were not lessened by being overlaid with Gothic horror: they were merely made fanciful. Blake knew, and shared, the faults of both manners. In his boyhood poem *To the Muses*, he set out the eighteenth-century manner with care and with charm, part parody and part pastiche, precisely in order to attack it.

> Whether on chrystal rocks ye rove,
>   Beneath the bosom of the sea
> Wand'ring in many a coral grove,
>   Fair Nine, forsaking Poetry!
>
> How have you left the antient love
>   That bards of old enjoy'd in you!
> The languid strings do scarcely move!
>   The sound is forc'd, the notes are few!   11

And the Gothic misuse taught Blake, as sharply as Coleridge, to distinguish its fabulous fancy from a living imagination of a piece with the thought.

> Fable or Allegory are a totally distinct & inferior kind of Poetry. Vision or Imagination is a Representation of what Eternally Exists, Really & Unchangeably. Fable or Allegory is Form'd by the daughters of Memory. Imagination is surrounded by the daughters of Inspiration.   604

In Gray, in Walpole, in Percy, the Gothic violence was out of place because it was unreal. Burke in the Commons raged of 'the Birds of Prey and Passage', 'the Orang-Outang or the Tiger'—

> The cries of India are given to seas and winds to be blown about, in every breaking up of the monsoon, over a remote and unhearing ocean.

The members who sidled out could not be blamed for finding this unreal, from a man whose family deals in India were known to be shady. They found the kindred rhetoric of Wesley as embarrassing, and believed it to be as hypocritical. They were mistaken. The 'Vulgar Enthusiasm' of the revivalists was more hysterical than the Gothic horror; but it was real. Put beside Burke the writers of the great evangelical hymns, say Cowper:

> God moves in a mysterious way,
>   His wonders to perform;
> He plants his footsteps in the sea,
>   And rides upon the storm.

The grandiloquence speaks no more than it believes; and, believing this, it speaks almost humbly. So Isaac Watts had spoken, in *Our God, Our Help in Ages past*. The more fleshly language which these men also spoke was no less real, and no less apt. The violence of Watts in *The Day of Judgment* is purposeful.

> Hark the shrill Outcries of the guilty Wretches!
> Lively bright Horror and amazing Anguish
> Stare thro' their Eye-lids, while the living Worm lies
>   Gnawing within them.
> Thoughts like old Vultures prey upon their Heartstrings,
> And the Smart twinges, when their Eye beholds the
> Lofty Judge frowning, and a Flood of Vengeance
>   Rolling afore him.
> Hopeless Immortals! how they scream and shiver
> While Devils push them to the Pit wide yawning
> Hideous and gloomy, to receive them headlong
>   Down to the Centre.

This is the imagery which Blake took up in *Night the Ninth, being The Last Judgment* of *Vala or The Four Zoas*. He knew the same spectacular imagery in the work of the evangelical sculptors, Bacon and Flaxman, who brought back the Cross, the Angel, and the Flaming Sword. It is the imagery which made John Wesley's preaching at once moving and horrifying.

Because this is an imagery of the flesh, the satirists tattled of the women who had fainted for Watts and who fainted with Wesley. They found its hysteria blasphemous. We should think Charles Wesley's *Wrestling Jacob* a blasphemous poem.

> 'Tis all in vain to hold thy Tongue,
>   Or touch the Hollow of my Thigh:
> Though every Sinew be unstrung,
>   Out of my Arms Thou shalt not fly;
> Wrestling I will not let Thee go,
> Till I thy Name, thy Nature know.

And Blake's prophetic books show that it is an imagery which lends itself to excess. But it remains an imagery of a piece with its thought. And, direct and powerful, it could sweep channels clear as glass. It did so in Blake's poems, childish in innocence but with a grown bodily urgency. The most searching and steady symbols in Blake are the symbols of the Sunday school. Nineteenth-century poets lost more than innocence when they put them aside, for that imagery of the Sunday picnic which, in a few years of childhood, had been Wordsworth's actual nature.

TWO

Begin from the wording of some simple hymn: say, from John Wesley's words—

> 'Tis mercy all, that thou hast brought
> My mind to seek her peace in thee.

This goes straight into the *Songs of Innocence*—

> To Mercy, Pity, Peace, and Love
> All pray in their distress;
> And to these virtues of delight
> Return their thankfulness.
>   For Mercy, Pity, Peace, and Love
> Is God, our father dear,
> And Mercy, Pity, Peace, and Love
> Is Man, his child and care.   117

If Blake had stopped here, it would not have been worth following him even so far. He goes on:

> For Mercy has a human heart,
> Pity a human face,
> And Love, the human form divine,
> And Peace, the human dress.
>   Then every man, of every clime,
> That prays in his distress,
> Prays to the human form divine,
> Love, Mercy, Pity, Peace.
>   And all must love the human form,

> In heathen, turk, or jew;
> Where Mercy, Love, & Pity dwell
> There God is dwelling too.   117

Here the poem ends, as Blake etched it. But the thought was not ended. Blake recalled snatches of it many times, in verses such as those on Fuseli, 'both Turk & Jew'. But he followed fully two lines of the thought, to the contrary of the *Songs of Experience*.

One line begins at the name which Blake gave to this poem. He underlined its human meaning, by calling it *The Divine Image*. He then drafted a contrary, *The Human Image*, and etched it as *The Human Abstract*, to show the same virtues grown inhuman in self-interest.

> Pity could be no more,
> If we did not make somebody poor;
> And Mercy no more could be,
> If all were as happy as we.
>   And mutual fear brings Peace,
> Till the selfish Loves increase.   174

But the virtues make an abstract less forceful than their images. Blake therefore followed another line, from the imagery alone of the poem. In the compact poem which he called *A Divine Image*, he gave a meaning to the symbols of the heart, the face, the form, and the dress, more terrible than that which he found in Swedenborg and the Jewish mystics.

> Cruelty has a Human Heart,
> And Jealousy a Human Face;
> Terror the Human Form Divine,
> And Secrecy the Human Dress.
>   The Human Dress is forged Iron,
> The Human Form a fiery Forge,
> The Human Face a Furnace seal'd,
> The Human Heart its hungry Gorge.   221

These contraries show the movement from the *Songs of Innocence* to the *Songs of Experience*. It is the movement of many such pairs of poems: from *The Ecchoing Green* to *The Garden of Love*; from one to the other of the two *Nurse's Songs*; of the two *Holy Thursdays*; and of the two poems *The Chimney Sweeper*. But they show also that Blake was at pains to check this, when it took too glibly the air of a social movement. The most powerful images here are those which make of the body a forge and a furnace, in *A Divine Image* of new harshness. Blake etched this poem for the *Songs of Experience*, about 1794. But he knew that this iron imagery belonged to another world, in which his contraries were distorted to a social contrast. Blake marked out the world of the *Songs of Innocence and of Experience* firmly, when he chose to leave *A Divine Image* out of it.

Blake had etched the last of the *Songs of Innocence* in 1789, in that happy child mood which the French Revolution seemed to fulfil. There had been no contrary and no progression in his mind then. These were set out fully, in *The Marriage of Heaven and Hell*, after 1790. Blake was then etching the *Songs of Experience*, which he finished in 1794. The contrary was prompted by social bitterness. But it was the contrary not to social but to spiritual innocence. To be just, it must remain a contrary within the soul. Blake never retreated to the easy contrast of soul and body. Under the common name, *Songs of Innocence and of Experience*, he wrote of their world precisely, 'Shewing the two contrary states of the human soul'. The happy world of the *Songs of Innocence* had been a state of mind. The unhappy world of the *Songs of Experience* is the contrary state, thrust upon the mind by the English opposition to the French Revolution. The state which the *Songs of Experience* attack is the mind of the hypocrite. The symbol of innocence had been the child. The symbol of experience, mazy and manifold as the hypocrite, and as fascinating, is the father.

THREE

Of roughly fifty poems in the *Songs of Innocence and of Experience*, roughly twenty are written about a child. Six of these are about a child lost and found. These six poems are coupled to make three pairs, of which one pair stands in the *Songs of Innocence*, and two stand in the *Songs of Experience*. Their contraries are less simple than those of other paired poems, set one against the other in the *Songs of Innocence* and the *Songs of Experience*. For the story of the child lost and found is not a simple story. In it, Blake

debated most fully the progression which child and father are born
to make.

It begins in the *Songs of Innocence* at the story of *Erlkönig,*
which Blake had already told in *An Island in the Moon. The Little
Boy Lost* has followed a vapour, mistaking it for his father. *The
Little Boy Found* is led back to his searching mother by God, who
has taken the same father shape. There is a hint that the child has
been misled by that false self which Blake called the Spectre, and
is guided to that true self which Blake called the Emanation. These
are commonly male and female: although Blake came to turn
against the mother, from whom he had already taken away the
happy *Nurse's Song* which had been hers in *An Island in the Moon.*
But the meaning of the story here is simple. The child is led astray
and aright, both in following the father: he cannot do otherwise.
To him, the innocent, experience false and true has needs the same
shape.

The second pair of such poems is called *The Little Girl Lost* and
The Little Girl Found. The names are odd: for the child is no
longer lost.

> Leopards, tygers, play
> Round her as she lay,
> While the lion old
> Bow'd his mane of gold
>   And her bosom lick,
> And upon her neck
> From his eyes of flame
> Ruby tears there came;
>   While the lioness
> Loos'd her slender dress,
> And naked they convey'd
> To caves the sleeping maid.   113

Now her parents wander mistakenly after a false image.

> Tired and woe-begone,
> Hoarse with making moan,
> Arm in arm seven days
> They trac'd the desart ways.
>   Seven nights they sleep
> Among shadows deep,

> And dream they see their child
> Starv'd in desart wild.
>   Pale, thro' pathless ways
> The fancied image strays
> Famish'd, weeping, weak,
> With hollow piteous shriek.   11

Their vision of fear becomes a lion, and he, god-like, becomes 'A Spirit arm'd in gold' to lead them aright, to the child. For it is the parents who are found: experience has been guided back to inno cence: and there 'to this day they dwell', untroubled by 'the wolvish howl' of a world of beasts.

Blake is telling the contrary story to that of the boy lost and found. Therefore he moved these poems from the *Songs of Inno cence*, for which they had first been etched, to the *Songs of Experi ence*. The story is still simple; but the shift marks a new depth. In the *Songs of Innocence* this had been a gay fable of Rousseau's world of noble savagery. It had commonly been followed by a nursery poem of Christ, 'Little Lamb, who made thee?' Now Blake put this story beside a poem which asks the same question with another force:

> Tyger! Tyger! burning bright
> In the forests of the night,
> What immortal hand or eye
> Could frame thy fearful symmetry?   214

Once the lion had learnt to lie down with the lamb. But now the child, the lamb of God—

> I a child, & thou a lamb,
> We are called by his name   115

—must learn to lead her parents home to the Tygers of Wrath: 'The wrath of the lion is the wisdom of God'. Christ is become the Tyger, symbol of energy burning in a darkening world. It is no longer enough for the innocent boy to go from false experience to true, by chance. Experience itself must learn, fasting in the desert, to follow a greater innocence, by choice. What began as a fable in the child cult has become, in its new setting, a searching test of faith.

Was Jesus Humble? or did he
Give any proofs of Humility?
When but a Child he ran away
And left his Parents in dismay.
When they had wander'd three days long
These were the words upon his Tongue:
'No Earthly Parents I confess:
I am doing my Father's business.'
When the rich learned Pharisee
Came to consult him secretly,
Upon his heart with Iron pen
He wrote, 'Ye must be born again'.   750

The roaring of lions, the howling of wolves, the raging of the
stormy sea, and the destructive sword, are portions of eternity,
too great for the eye of man.   151

What the hammer? What the chain?
In what furnace was thy brain?
What the anvil? what dread grasp
Dare its deadly terrors clasp?
    When the stars threw down their spears,
And water'd heaven with their tears,
Did he smile his work to see?
Did he who made the Lamb make thee?   214

FOUR

Innocence which has thus been doubled on itself, to become fulfilment, will master nature. But to do so, it must master that false
experience whose form is fixed in societies. Blake put these two
sentences precisely:

The harvest shall flourish in wintry weather
When two virginities meet together:
    The King & the Priest must be tied in a tether
Before two virgins can meet together.   177

And this is the ready meaning of the last two of the poems of the
lost child: A *Little Boy Lost* and A *Little Girl Lost*, in the *Songs of*

Experience. Both poems are frank in social indignation. 'Are such things done on Albion's shore?' asks one; and the other answers:

> Children of the future Age
> Reading this indignant page,
> Know that in a former time
> Love! sweet Love! was thought a crime.   219

In both, and throughout the *Songs of Experience,* society is seen as a spiritual mutilation. The father has become one with the priest, and his love has grown rigid in jealousy.

> To her father white
> Came the maiden bright;
> But his loving look,
> Like the holy book,
> All her tender limbs with terror shook.   219

> Selfish father of men!
> Cruel, jealous, selfish fear!
> Can delight,
> Chain'd in night,
> The virgins of youth and morning bear?   211

For now the lost children are not found again: they are destroyed. The boy has preached natural love to his father, like Christ and like Cordelia, and the priest burns him. The girl has made love frankly with this or another boy, and her father casts her off. Both children begin in thoughtless innocence, making no judgement of experience false or true: as did the boy of the *Songs of Innocence.* Both then try to win their father to love, as did the girl whom Blake moved from the *Songs of Innocence* to the *Songs of Experience.* But now, both children fail; and they are destroyed. Innocence and experience have found for progression the crucifying hypocrite.

Blake wrote out this bitter progression a number of times. He did so fully in the poem *Infant Sorrow,* which he chose to follow *A Little Boy Lost.* Consider how Blake first wrote this poem in the commonplace book which he kept after the death of his brother Robert (it had been Robert's drawing-book) from about 1790 to about 1818, and which Rossetti later owned. There the poem begins at innocence unable to judge experience:

My mother groan'd, my father wept;
Into the dangerous world I leapt,
Helpless, naked, piping loud,
Like a fiend hid in a cloud.
  Struggling in my father's hands
Striving against my swaddling bands,
Bound & weary, I thought best
To sulk upon my mother's breast.   166

Innocence hopes to lead experience back to love and to delight.

When I saw that rage was vain,
And to sulk would nothing gain,
Turning many a trick & wile,
I began to soothe & smile.
  And I sooth'd day after day
Till upon the ground I stray;
And I smil'd night after night,
Seeking only for delight.   167

But innocence fails. The trees of sensuous experience for which it reached in hope are also those on which it is crucified.

And I saw before me shine
Clusters of the wand'ring vine,
And many a lovely flower & tree
Stretch'd their blossoms out to me.
  My father then with holy look,
In his hands a holy book,
Pronounc'd curses on my head
And bound me in a mirtle shade.   167

There is a meaning in which the whole progression lies coiled in the first helplessness: as always in Blake, 'within that Center Eternity expands Its ever during doors'. Therefore Blake was content to cut the poem to its first eight lines, in the *Songs of Experience*. And there is a meaning in which the progression unwinds over itself again and again. So Blake unwound it in *The Mental Traveller*, moving from child to parent and thence to child again, endlessly. But these are not the deepest meanings. They are more shallow than the hypocrite; for they miss the oneness of innocence with experience. Blake went on to write of this oneness fully.

M

FIVE

In Blake's commonplace book there is a poem *In a Mirtle Shade*, whose name designedly echoes the last words of *Infant Sorrow*. Here we read straight on, from the crucifixion to the resurrection.

> Why should I be bound to thee,
> O my lovely mirtle tree?
> Love, free love, cannot be bound
> To any tree that grows on ground.
>   O, how sick & weary I
> Underneath my mirtle lie,
> Like to dung upon the ground
> Underneath my mirtle bound.
>   Oft my mirtle sigh'd in vain
> To behold my heavy chain;
> Oft my father saw us sigh,
> And laugh'd at our simplicity.
>   So I smote him & his gore
> Stain'd the roots my mirtle bore.
> But the time of youth is fled,
> And grey hairs are on my head.   169

In few poems do the layers of thought and symbol grow together so closely. It is well to look at them as closely.

Blake wrote out the first lines of this poem again, adding one image: that the mirtle is 'Blossoms show'ring all around'. The child had reached for the shower of blossoms in *Infant Sorrow*, and had been forbidden it. Recall what Blake wrote of this longing elsewhere in his commonplace book.

> I fear'd the fury of my wind
> Would blight all blossoms fair & true;
> And my sun it shin'd & shin'd
> And my wind it never blew.
>   But a blossom fair or true
> Was not found on any tree;
> For all blossoms grew & grew
> Fruitless, false, tho' fair to see.   166

This is one meaning of *In a Mirtle Shade*: that experience alone can make fruitful the blossoms for which innocence longed. The mirtle-tree has yielded only blossoms, because only the child has been offered to it, as another kind of fertilizer, 'like to dung upon the ground'. To become fruitful, the mirtle must be fertilized thus by the father: 'his gore Stain'd the roots my mirtle bore'. The murder of the father is the wind of wrath in which alone tree and child can fulfil themselves.

Yet the tree itself is not a simple symbol of delight. In another meaning it is the father's deadly heritage to the child. The tree has always been the cross. To it are bound those suffering gods who are children, the shifting heroes of Blake's prophetic books. But the tree springs up, only when they are bound. The jealous Los binds Orc in *Night the Fifth* of *Vala or The Four Zoas*; and when he repents, he finds that Orc has become a tree. This tree is the life in the senses alone: Blake called that one-sided life, the Vegetated Spectre. It is kin to A *Poison Tree* of deceit in the *Songs of Experience*, and to the tree in *The Human Abstract* at which, like Eve, man learns to play the hypocrite.

> The Gods of the earth and sea
> Sought thro' Nature to find this Tree;
> But their search was all in vain:
> There grows one in the Human Brain.   217

Blake linked this tree with the gallows, because it is 'Moral Virtue and the Law', the tree of Mystery of state religion. Gallows and Cross alike, it is a tree which we all must bear. Although the life in the senses is one-sided, it is part of the whole life, innocence and experience together; and only by way of this life can we enter a whole life. The tree is the knowledge of good and evil. The child is freed from the tree only when these are become one.

For he is freed by murder. It is the deepest meaning of *In a Mirtle Shade*, that innocence becomes experience by energy; and to that end must submit to becoming guilty, because it must work in the flesh. This is the full round of Blake's progression: when the child, in killing the father, has become a father:

> But the time of youth is fled,
> And grey hairs are on my head.   169

The round returns on the shower of blossoms; the father of A *Little Girl Lost* knew

O, the trembling fear!
O, the dismal care!
That shakes the blossoms of my hoary hair.   219

This is the brave interplay, of selfless energy submitting to itself, and of the spirit fined in the father furnace until he bursts it, which makes Blake's gravest poems. Two passages from *Vala or The Four Zoas* are apt.

What is the price of Experience? do men buy it for a song?
Or wisdom for a dance in the street? No, it is bought with the price
Of all that a man hath, his house, his wife, his children.
Wisdom is sold in the desolate market where none come to buy,
And in the wither'd field where the farmer plows for bread in vain.   290

[Unorganiz'd Innocence: An Impossibility.]
Innocence dwells with Wisdom, but never with Ignorance.   380

SIX

It becomes plain that Blake in his commonplace book saw good and evil less simply divided than they had been in the *Songs of Innocence and of Experience*. For the *Songs of Experience* are, at bottom, songs of indignation. We seem to see them so clearly, lying below their fluid grace, that we are not always aware that the grace is acid: the fluid etches. In these songs experience takes many forms: Newtonian rationalism 'the starry floor'; materialism 'the wat'ry shore'; religion the mystery; jealousy the thorny rose, cankered by self-love: and every form mutilates. Blake is going back to the beginning of the child cult, to see society itself as the mutilating force. The poem *To Tirzah*, which Blake added seven or eight years after the other *Songs of Experience* had been etched, has the air even of dividing the spirit from the body. We are turned back to John Wesley's hymn, from which we began:

O hide this self from me, that I
No more, but Christ in me may live;

> My vile affections crucify,
>   Nor let one darling lust survive;
> In all things nothing may I see,
>   Nothing desire or seek but thee.

This is innocence and experience, not in progression, but in plain
negation. And innocence is then not an energy which remakes man,
but a passive grace which is given him, to ease his restlessness.

> 'Tis mercy all, that thou hast brought
>   My mind to seek her peace in thee;
> Yet while I seek, but find thee not,
>   No peace my wand'ring soul shall see;
> O when shall all my wand'rings end,
>   And all my steps to thee-ward tend!

This is not a divinity in which Blake could rest. Even the *Songs
of Experience*, founded on such hymns, go beyond it. But the progression which the motto to *To Tirzah* seeks, to raise 'a Spiritual
Body', is reached only in Blake's commonplace book. It is reached
in the most remarkable of Blake's symbols, good and evil wedded
as one, and always loathed but always again fascinating: the
hypocrite.

About the time that he was etching the *Songs of Experience*, in
1793, Blake engraved a picture-book for children, which he called
The Gates of Paradise. About 1818 he printed this book again, and
added to it some of the last verses which he wrote. They set
squarely against Wesley's divinity 'of Sin & stern Repentance' a
greater divinity:

> Mutual Forgiveness of each Vice,
> Such are the Gates of Paradise.   761

This is the generosity of a man whom a lifetime of experience has
remade, innocent. And, more telling than in such formal sentences,
it speaks easily, patiently, with grave good humour, even to those
whom lifetimes have taught nothing. So Blake, coming back to this
early book at the end of his poetic life, speaks *To The Accuser who
is The God of This World*.

> Truly, My Satan, thou art but a Dunce,
> And dost not know the Garment from the Man.

> Every Harlot was a Virgin once,
> Nor can'st thou ever change Kate into Nan.
>   Tho' thou art Worship'd by the Names Divine
> Of Jesus & Jehovah, thou art still
> The Son of Morn in weary Night's decline,
> The lost Traveller's Dream under the Hill.   771

Satan is become one with another symbol of the hypocrite, the Angel: 'Messiah or Satan or Tempter'. And, uneasy between good in *The Marriage of Heaven and Hell* and evil in *Milton*, Satan has found his place. For the hypocrite is the wrongdoer who knows his wrong, and is therefore the silent witness to the knowledge of right.

> To be an Error & to be Cast out is a part of God's design.
> No man can Embrace True Art till he has Explor'd & cast out
> False Art (such is the Nature of Mortal Things).   613

Therefore the lost Traveller must dream of him: the lost child must learn that behind the vapour stands God the father, in the same shape. They must learn by choice, not by chance: 'Whenever any Individual Rejects Error & Embraces Truth, a Last Judgment passes upon that Individual.' The hypocrite is the crux and symbol of choice; and Blake can write of him with the ripeness of a man happy in the choice of right. Turn from Satan to the hypocrite Angel, in Blake's commonplace book.

> I asked a thief to steal me a peach:
> He turned up his eyes.
> I ask'd a lithe lady to lie her down:
> Holy & meek she cries.
>   As soon as I went an angel came:
> He wink'd at the thief
> And smil'd at the dame,
> And without one word spoke
> Had a peach from the tree,
> And 'twixt earnest & joke
> Enjoy'd the Lady.   163

Blake rewrote this poem in a number of ways, to underline the hypocrisy of its story. He made the lady give herself 'still as a maid', with that contempt for mock chasteness which he wrote out in the lines *On the Virginity of the Virgin Mary & Johanna*

Southcott. But the contempt does not turn the poem into one of social surrender. For we must not read the poem as a bitter joke, that Blake is helpless where the angel is deft. Certainly the joke is against Blake; but the joke is that he is clumsy rather than helpless; and it is a good joke. To understand it, we should read with this another poem which Blake wrote in his commonplace book at the same time, about 1793.

> Never seek to tell thy love
> Love that never told can be;
> For the gentle wind does move
> Silently, invisibly.
>   I told my love, I told my love,
> I told her all my heart,
> Trembling, cold, in ghastly fears –
> Ah, she doth depart.
>   Soon as she was gone from me
> A traveller came by
> Silently, invisibly –
> O, was no deny.   161

This is the same poem as *I asked a thief*; the changes which Blake made in it underline the sameness. In both poems Blake shows himself to fail because he makes love too honestly: he speaks. He does not think himself wrong in this; yet neither is the traveller wrong, to play the hypocrite angel. This is not merely how the world is: it is how the world must be—unyielding to those who remain 'trembling, cold'. Like the angel, the traveller from childhood to manhood must learn to work within man himself, to remake experience into innocence 'still as a maid'. The soul must submit to be made one and fruitful, sense and mind together, from man's own contraries. And only the wind makes fruitful, 'silently, invisibly'. Fully to savour Blake's graceful angel, eating his peach in Paradise before the Fall, we must meet him in *A Vision of the Last Judgment*.

> The Player is a liar when he says: 'Angels are happier than Men because they are better.' Angels are happier than Men & Devils because they are not always Prying after Good & Evil in one another & eating the Tree of Knowledge for Satan's Gratification.   616

But the hypocrite is earnest as well as joke. As witness to choice, he is also the tool of judgement. Therefore Blake writes of Chaucer's Pardoner, 'the Age's Knave':

> This man is sent in every age for a rod and scourge, and for a blight, for a trial of men, to divide the classes of men; he is in the most holy sanctuary, and he is suffered by Providence for wise ends, and has also his great use, and his grand leading destiny.
>
> His companion, the Sompnour, is also a Devil of the first magnitude, grand, terrific, rich and honoured in the rank of which he holds the destiny. The uses to Society are perhaps equal of the Devil and of the Angel, their sublimity, who can dispute.   570

SEVEN

Blake wrote poems for perhaps fifty years of his life. He had begun as a boy to count out ten syllables to a line of the *Poetical Sketches*. And even those painstaking lines gather an astonishing speed and liveliness of rhythm.

> The hills tell each other, and the list'ning
> Vallies hear; all our longing eyes are turned
> Up to thy bright pavillions: issue forth,
> And let thy holy feet visit our clime.   1

He ended with the grave and easy speech of *The Everlasting Gospel* and of the lines *To The Accuser who is The God of This World*. In all his poems the speech is one with the thought, lucid and searching, a writing richer than the prophetic books. The oneness is a model for his own progressions: the sensuous with the reasoning, Rousseau with Voltaire; innocence with experience, the child and the world remaking one another. Nothing shows Blake's insight so plainly as to watch him remake one of his visions to such a progression.

When Blake moved to Felpham in 1800 Butts sent him some genteel verses of good wishes; and Blake dutifully sent back some verses of vision, as genteel. The vision on the Felpham sands is drab and laboured. But there is a moment in it when Blake sees

'a World in a Grain of Sand' with all the Minute Particulars of
true imagery; and the mild landscape is suddenly struck alight and
alive.

> In particles bright
> The jewels of Light
> Distinct shone & clear.
> Amaz'd & in fear
> I each particle gazed,
> Astonish'd, Amazed;
> For each was a Man
> Human-form'd.   804

In his prophetic books Blake is at pains to fit such thoughts to
the shape of his world construct: 'She also took an Atom of Space,
with dire pain opening it a Center Into Beulah.' But in his poems
Blake does not miss the dazzling moment. The sand—

> Abstinence sows sand all over
> The ruddy limbs & flaming hair   178

—taking on the Human Form Divine; the sand breaking the light
into the particles of Newton's *Opticks*, yet shining like the faces
of men who have been blessed,

> That in blessing I will bless thee, and in multiplying I will
> multiply thy seed as the stars of the heaven, and as the sand
> which is upon the sea shore:

this is an instant of imagination, holding together two contraries
of thought, in which the reasoner is suddenly turned to good as
surely as the man of passion. The curse of a mechanical rationalism
becomes a fruitful blessing in the senses, as the curse of Balaam had
been made to bless—

> How goodly are thy tents, O Jacob, and thy tabernacles,
> O Israel! As the valleys are they spread forth, as gardens
> by the river's side, as the trees of lign aloes which the Lord
> hath planted, and as cedar trees beside the waters.

All this Blake could see, could seize, and could pack into a single
poem of contraries, the light breaking and enlarging from image
to image, with a precision and a generosity which puts the prophetic

books to shame. He wrote nothing else so sure as the poem in his commonplace book which he made from this:

> Mock on, Mock on Voltaire, Rousseau:
> Mock on, Mock on: 'tis all in vain!
> You throw the sand against the wind,
> And the wind blows it back again.
>   And every sand becomes a Gem
> Reflected in the beams divine;
> Blown back they blind the mocking Eye,
> But still in Israel's paths they shine.
>   The Atoms of Democritus
> And Newton's Particles of light
> Are sands upon the Red sea shore,
> Where Israel's tents do shine so bright.   418

The ease and peace are the patient goods of a man who has reached his own progression. And they are more moving at last even than the noble indignation of the *Songs of Experience*. The hypocrite world has fulfilled itself, in its own despite. 'Error is Created. Truth is Eternal.' But man knows the one only by the other. He lives by making, even though he makes only mistakes. 'To be an Error & to be Cast out is a part of God's design.'

THE MAN WITHOUT A MASK

ONE

William Blake lived in the most violent age of English history. Its revolution had indeed long been gathering speed. Industry was grouping itself afresh, the new farming had been begun, the population was growing, before Blake was born. Nevertheless, England then thought herself, and had remained, a country whose world trade was founded in the village. It was overwhelmingly in Blake's lifetime that industry moved to the factory; that farming enlarged its scale; and that iron and coal gave England her new skeleton. When Blake was born, the population of England was less than seven millions. It had doubled before he died. The cost of living more than doubled; wages did not. And through all these years walked the ironmaster war. Blake was born in the Seven Years' War. He learned to think as a man during the American War. His years of promise were turned to defeat in the war against the French Revolution, from 1793 to 1802. Defeat deepened to poverty and bitterness in the war against Napoleon, from 1803 to 1815. 'We have Hirelings in the Camp, the Court & the University, who would, if they could, for ever depress Mental & prolong Corporeal War.' And this war did not end at Waterloo. The Sedition Acts, the Combination Laws, the suspension of Habeas Corpus were still riding with the yeomanry against the Manchester suffrage meeting at St Peter's Field on 16 August 1819. England knew what the wars had meant when she called this massacre Peterloo. In that year Cobbett, bringing Paine's bones home to England, found for welcome the Six Acts, more savage than Pitt's

Sedition Acts. A year before Blake died, Lancashire had its worst slump, and starving mobs broke a thousand power looms in three days. Half a dozen years after he died, the Reform Bill, the Factory Act, and the new Poor Law had made the factory owners masters of England.

Blake lived through the birth of the world which we know. He felt its pangs in his life. A craftsman in a world worked by women and children; a dissenter in the world of the Holy Alliance; a workman in a world of booming profits: he was such a poet as no age before his could have made, and no age since has made. Others had begun with his hopes: Wordsworth, Coleridge, and Southey. In the 1790s the Government had found no writer more able than George Canning to rhyme for it in *The Anti-Jacobin*. One by one the Jacobins retreated. Wordsworth took a sinecure. Coleridge proclaimed himself heir to Burke. Southey had been the main butt of William Gifford, who edited *The Anti-Jacobin*. Such lesser butts as Lamb and Hazlitt never forgave Gifford. But Southey became a writer for the Tory *Quarterly Review*, under Gifford's editorship. These men did not hide the fears which drove them. In 1812 Southey was writing of the French Revolution for the *Quarterly Review*; and told Walter Scott that the writing was

> most mournfully well timed. At this moment nothing but the Army preserves us from the most dreadful of all calamities, an insurrection of the poor against the rich, and how long the Army may be depended upon is a question which I scarcely dare to ask myself.

Next year Southey took the laureateship, which Gray and Hayley before, and Scott then, had thought beneath them. He was angry when one of his youthful plays of revolt was reprinted in 1817; and the House of Commons was angrier.

Blake alone did not sink to the outlook of these men, that their society was a fortress beleaguered by the poor. He went on hating King Hunger more than King Ludd, and governments more than crowds. To him, it was the society which wronged the Human Form Divine. The manufacturing poor were indeed misshapen and frightening: because like others they had been mutilated.

> Because of the Opressors of Albion in every City & Village.

> They mock at the Labourer's limbs: they mock at his
> starv'd Children.   656
>
> All the marks remain of the slave's scourge & tyrant's
> Crown,
> And of the Priest's o'ergorged Abdomen, & of the mer-
> chant's thin
> Sinewy deception, & of the warrior's outbraving &
> thoughtlessness
> In lineaments too extended & in bones too strait & long.
> They shew their wounds: they accuse.   363

This passionate sympathy, loathing the moneyed world, opens
two ways into Blake's prophetic books. One way has taken us
from his political hopes to the secrecy and the helplessness which
come to baffle these books. Their thickening mystery and their
proliferation of chaos have a history: it is the history of the years
from 1791 to 1798. Blake could speak even his symbolic rhetoric
plainly, when he chose. That choice was never simple for him,
because his mind was at ease among shifting myths. Nevertheless,
he did choose to speak plainly in *The French Revolution* in 1791.
He did not cease to do so altogether for four years after. He
would not have gone back to mystery then, had it not chimed
with his thought. But the thought was prompted by censorship,
and urged by disaster. As we learn of the censorship of those dis-
astrous years, we cannot doubt that Blake believed what he wrote—

> To defend the Bible in this year 1798 would cost a man his
> life.
> The Beast & the Whore rule without control.   383

We cannot doubt that he acted as he believed—

> I have been commanded from Hell not to print this, as it is
> what our Enemies wish.   383

And to the Government censor was added a censor within: the
loss of hope in the French Revolution and in its politics. These
are worldly shadows which stand behind many mystics: the Pytha-
goreans, the early Christian Gnostics, the Manichaeans, the Albi-
genses, and even the Cabbalists of Spain. We may read their
whole context in four sentences in which Blake attacked the
kindred evils of religion and law.

> Angels are happier than Men & Devils because they are
> not always Prying after Good & Evil in one another & eating
> the Tree of Knowledge for Satan's Gratification.
>
> Thinking as I do that the Creator of this World is a very
> Cruel Being, & being a Worshipper of Christ, I cannot help
> saying: 'the Son, O how unlike the Father!' First God
> Almighty comes with a Thump on the Head. Then Jesus
> Christ comes with a balm to heal it.   617

For these are Gnostic heresies, in their social and in their spiritual
meanings.

There is another way into the prophetic books which Blake's
sympathy with his fellow workmen opens. As we read on in these
books, we grow aware that their imagery darkens. They come to
crowd with iron and machines, the wheel and the mill, the kiln,
the forge and the loom, at an endless task of building under a
furnace sky. We have followed this imagery into the Industrial
Revolution, made over from the craftsman's compasses to the mill-
wheel which unmans him.

> I stood among my valleys of the south
> And saw a flame of fire, even as a Wheel
> Of fire surrounding all the heavens: it went
> From west to east, against the current of
> Creation, and devour'd all things in its loud
> Fury & thundering course round heaven & earth.   717

This is the true horror, the fire and the web, the sulphur cloud
of the later prophetic books. It is a vision more vivid than the
eye's, that Blake saw the machine grow larger than man, to make
him stunted, ignorant, and beastly. The workmen drilling on the
moor by night were not alone in these fears. For Blake in his craft
shared their fate, 'in sorrowful drudgery to obtain a scanty pittance
of bread'; and shared their understanding. No one who has looked
afresh at the moving hackneyed lines at the head of *Milton* will
doubt that these were real to Blake, however far off and clouded
with the symbolism of the planetary mills of Newton.

> And did the Countenance Divine
> Shine forth upon our clouded hills?
> And was Jerusalem builded here
> Among these dark Satanic Mills?   481

For the Countenance Divine is the Divine Image, shining in Pity
the Human Face. No one who has seen Arkwright's mills still
standing, huge and gloomy, among the lonely Derbyshire hills
whose beauty was another of Blake's unseen visions, will doubt
the pity, the truth, and the urgency of his faith.

> I will not cease from Mental Fight,
> Nor shall my Sword sleep in my hand
> Till we have built Jerusalem
> In England's green & pleasant Land.   481

> Hear the voice of the Bard!
> Who Present, Past, & Future sees;
> Whose ears have heard
> The Holy Word
> That walk'd among the ancient trees,
>   Calling the lapsed Soul,
> And weeping in the evening dew;
> That might controll
> The starry pole,
> And fallen, fallen light renew!
>   'O Earth, O Earth, return!'   210

TWO

Blake's thought rested squarely on the world in which he lived.
The two revolutions which shook that world were actual in his
life, and are actual in his writings. Unless we see them there, we
cannot read his writings rightly; and shall find them eccentric,
as his life has been found eccentric. Blake's life was not eccentric,
whether Thomas Butts did once see him and his wife naked
while reading *Paradise Lost*, or whether he did not. We find it
eccentric, only if we miss its context, which is made by his writings
and his times together: the context of a man living in a public,
not a private, world. If we give our fancy to the privacy of a
man who gave his mind to living in public, we shall needs find
him eccentric; but the eccentricity is ours. The context of Blake's
writings is the context of a man who gave his mind to speaking
to a public world; and the man was of a piece. The public did not
listen. But it stood about the speaker.

N

We begin to read Blake's writings when we see the actual within them. But this is a beginning to reading; it is not an understanding and a judgement. Everything which Blake had in common with others is apt to his actual. It helps us to fix Blake. But it is not Blake. An able critic seems to have held that we understand Blake when we think that he was oversexed. This is a reasonable guess; the other reasonable guess is that he was undersexed. Both guesses are helpful. But Blake was one of a population numbering, as a mean, nearly ten million English men and women. It is a reasonable guess that, at any time in Blake's life, more than half a million of these were either oversexed or undersexed. It seems a pity that no others of them found time to write the *Songs of Innocence*. Or did they lack the gift? And if so, how much of Blake's gift was that he was oddly sexed?

There are other psychological placings which are as helpful; and no more helpful. Blake's lost child finds himself in *In a Mirtle Shade*, when he murders his father. Then, and then only, end the poems of the child lost and found. These poems, and others, carry a fear and a guilt, which are common in men who as boys were uneasy with their fathers. The shifting symbols, from the father priest to God the father, and from God's 'Thump on the Head' to 'the Son, O how unlike the Father,' point to the same uneasiness. It seems likely that Blake's feelings in childhood had conspired against his father. There are signs that, in manhood, they conspired against his wife. But these are fairly common feelings. It is helpful to recall them, because they remind us that Blake was a man like others. His thought begins with theirs. But we read Blake to-day because he was a man unlike others; and because his thought went on as theirs did not. It is well thus to look for the beginnings of Blake's thought, because they help us to know what shapes it could have taken. But of these shapes, Blake took the greater and rejected the less. We know the greater only from his writings. That Blake may have feared his father, and been restless with his wife, bounded his thought: it did not make it. Blake wrote searchingly of such feelings when he wrote of the patrons of his time—

> It is in their Power to hinder Instruction but not to Instruct, just as it is in their power to Murder a Man but not to make a Man.   597

There is indeed a kinship beteen the imagery of contraries in Blake and in the greater psycho-analysts. The kinship grows from kindred ways of looking at man: Spectre and Emanation, father and child, ego and id: the mask and the face. All are looking at man in society; and see him alike, because they see the root contraries, society bounding man. Seeing these contraries in the same industrial setting, all see them as famine against plenty. The poor have only one neurosis: insecurity, the fear of hunger. The rich build a wall of social niceties, and people it within as did Boccaccio's gallants in a year of plague, with spiritual famine: Desire Ungratified. Blake was as forthright against this as Freud.

> In a wife I would desire
> What in whores is always found –
> The lineaments of Gratified desire.
>
> Abstinence sows sand all over
> The ruddy limbs & flaming hair,
> But Desire Gratified
> Plants fruits of life & beauty there.   178

But Blake did not rest at that shallow contrary, of sex, of power, or of greed. These are not the ends of man in society; but are the means by which society cripples those at work, and poisons those at leisure. Blake believed that society has no ends. Like his machines, it is a means become master. He thought the more deeply of the ends of man.

THREE

What is true of Blake's psychological is true of his social outlook. Like others, Blake speaks the discontent of his time. Until we know the discontent, we do not begin to read his writings; because we do not speak their language. It is a noble language, and we should be proud that Blake shared it with Paine, with Priestley, and with William Hone. But a language is not yet the thing said. All these men spoke the same just discontent; but no two of them said the same thing. It is an odd bigotry, if we feel the social urges which drove these men, then to dismiss as private fancies the faiths to which they drove them. When we trace the

actual revolutions in Blake's writings we learn a new respect for
his mind. We learn that it was not the mind of a crank. But if
we then shrug away as a foible what that mind said besides, we
dishonour our respect. The search for origins and motives is a
tool. If we make it the end of our reading, if we grow impatient
of what stands on the page, we are not realist, but smug and
eccentric. And we make a caricature of Blake.

Blake's writings grew within the French Revolution and the
Industrial Revolution. In these, in the two kinds of rationalism,
and in the two kinds of dissent, lie the roots of his thought. From
these roots grew his dialectic of contraries and progression, some
form of which is common to all mystics. It grew in Blake in the
form most fitted to an industrial society. It took a like form in
Hegel and in Karl Marx. All three said like things with this
dialectic. But no two of them said the same thing. The dialectic
is striking. It is striking that Blake used it before the others. But
what was said comes to mean more than the language of the
dialectic. Marx found and said searching things with this dialectic,
which will remain worth reading. Hegel did not, and is unread.
Blake spoke in this language a thought which remains his own;
and it is worth the reading.

Blake's thought begins at the evil, that society thwarts the
fulfilment of man. Thus religion thwarts Christ: the thought is
Priestley's. Thus law thwarts Desire Gratified: the thought is
Franklin's. Thus, as Blake first saw, a man-made famine thwarts
the plenty which men make. Blake hated this blight, and fought
it his life long.

> Some say that Happiness is not Good for Mortals, & they
> ought to be answer'd that Sorrow is not fit for Immortals
> & is utterly useless to any one; a blight never does good to a
> tree, & if a blight kill not a tree but it still bear fruit, let none
> say that the fruit was in consequence of the blight.   830

And Blake knew that the blight must be fought within society. He
was neither bigot enough, nor so idle a well-wisher, to think that
man can make his good without that revolution. There must be
an end to wilful famine. Man must be set free, to make his good.
But he must still make his good, himself. It is not a grace given

to him, even by revolutions. They can give him the means to be good. They can free him from the drudgery, the fear, the rigours forbidding thought, and the hunt of beasts for the mere 'necessaries of animal life', with which a society cripples and distorts the very will to good. Revolutions can free him from self-interest: it is the thought which Marx made noble. But they have not then remade man; they have freed him to remake himself. The good remains an end to which societies can give means, but which man must know and must make.

For Blake, who knew that the French Revolution had made a better society, knew also that it had not made a good society. He did not believe that societies can be good. They can be means to good: as means, they can be better or worse: they can be good for an end, and for a time; but, because they are means, they cannot be good, in themselves. Blake did not shirk the contraries, from his society to a better society. He did not lack the fire raging against content, and raging to remake society, not to-morrow but to-day. But Blake did not shirk the heavier knowledge, that a society remade will remain a society to be remade. The society remade will take on the same rigour of death, unless in turn it submits to progress through its new contrary. The contraries of thesis and antithesis do not end. The progression to synthesis is not made by one revolution, in France or in the world. This is the full meaning of the dialectic of contraries, in Blake and in Marx: that no revolution is the last. This is a heavy thought, but it is a living thought, that societies live only as they are remade. It is the burning thought of Blake's energy, making and remaking, and urgent always with the will to good.

FOUR

This thought at last sets society against man, because each society fails to be that good which its men fought to fulfil. But it is also a generous thought, seeing in men a will to good which they deny only because they have been mutilated. The generosity shines in the symbol of the hypocrite, which moved Blake to anger, to loathing, and to hope, at once. For it is not enough that the will to good is innocent. Innocence is helpless. Even the hypocrite is a more powerful witness to good, because his judgement has grown in experience. The will to good must be driven by experience. The progressions of societies are endless, and perhaps the hypocrite is the catalyst whose stifled discontent sets off that ferment. But the contraries of innocence and experience close, in the progression to an innocence wise and fruitful by experience. The child must take, and must murder, experience; it must become father and hypocrite; and it will have found itself if that iron cruelty has rewritten innocence. The symbol is iron.

> When the rich learned Pharisee
> Came to consult him secretly,
> Upon his heart with Iron pen
> He wrote, 'Ye must be born again'.   750

This is the peace of progression which man must seek in societies, but must make in himself. For this, Blake wished to set him free from the evils of his age. Only in this peace could be made the whole man: not sense nor reason alone, and not the negation of either, but the progression to the soul itself, in the imagination which is man and God together.

> Imagination is the Divine Vision not of The World, or of
> Man, nor from Man as he is a Natural Man, but only as he is
> a Spiritual Man.   783

This is the faith of every great poet from Philip Sidney to Blake. It is the deeper faith in Blake, because he is both the mystic seeking the one in the many and the revolutionary seeking man in his societies. Both speak together when Blake writes,

> God only Acts & Is, in existing beings or Men.   155
> Therefore God becomes as we are, that we may be as he
> is.   98

And both seek the same man in himself, and the same ideal in the renewing life and death of societies, in *A Vision of the Last Judgment*. 'Error is Created. Truth is Eternal.'

This is an anti-social ideal; but it is not an ideal which therefore withdraws from society. Blake did withdraw, for reasons which are plain and pitiful in his poverty and in his fears. But he spoke this ideal forcefully for twenty years before he withdrew. He shared it with such men as Richard Price, who never withdrew. For Blake's ideal is not single and ascetic but is part of his lively dialectic. The crux of that dialectic is, that all societies fall short of man's good; but that men cannot be good, because they cannot be themselves, outside society. What is done always distorts what has been imagined. But what has been imagined must be given a shape by doing, and is not fully imagined until it has been done. This is the progression of innocence and experience, murdering one another. It is the progression between a society and the way of living which it seeks to fix. And it is the progression between the poem and its imagination. To take one side or other of these contraries: to hold that the social man is prompted by social forces alone; or that he who knows that the poem always speaks the thought awry must needs be dumb: this is to miss the movement of Blake's contraries to progression. Innocence returns to itself, greater, by way of experience. Blake's ideal is the imaginative soul. But that Divine Vision must work in the world: God cannot reveal himself without Urizen, the physical creator. 'God only Acts & Is, in existing beings or Men.' And though the ideal errs in the hypocrite world, 'to be an Error & to be Cast out is a part of God's design'.

FIVE

Against the proliferation of error which the vegetable world renews, Blake saw a single soul in the imagination. It was to him the likeness of God in the body of man. Blake saw it with the humanity with which he had marked Lavater's first *Aphorisms*, and which he wrote out himself.

> As all men are alike in outward form, So (and with the same infinite variety) all are alike in the Poetic Genius.   98

> That call'd Body is a portion of Soul discern'd by the five Senses, the chief inlets of Soul in this age.   149

That is, Blake saw the soul as that which is lasting and common in men, of which their common shape is one form: the Human Form Divine. The soul within is as the body without, that which makes man himself and not another animal. Blake looked for man's fulfilment in that which at last makes him man alone, and alone makes him man: the sum of his mind, his feelings, his dignity, his knowledge of truth and of love, his reason in the widest meaning: his belief in his own imagination. The imagination sets the worth for which societies reach and fail: pity and justice, order and happiness, peace with passion. It is the worth which man knows, for it is *The Divine Image.*

> Mercy has a human heart,
> Pity a human face,
> And Love, the human form divine,
> And Peace, the human dress.
>   Then every man, of every clime,
> That prays in his distress,
> Prays to the human form divine,
> Love, Mercy, Pity, Peace.   117

Yet could Blake believe truly that these are held in common by every man, of every clime and time? Man himself is not the same man everywhere and always. His societies change him as he changes them; and the glacier-slow movements of nature change both together. We may agree to put aside the fearful changes which poverty and indignity work. These are the mutilations which most men suffer; but they remain mutilations, of the true man whom we wish to make and remember. But even that free, whole, and living man changes. Then do not his truths and ideals change with him? We share truths with Homer and the Bible, with Buddha and the Aztecs. But it is unlikely that we share them with Neanderthal man, and fairly certain that we do not share them with the ape and the sponge. Man has outgrown his cave drawings. He will outgrow the ideals of Plato and the innocence of Blake. What truths can be stable in the soul of man, so easily mutilated, by nature so changeable?

I do not put these questions because I think them apt: I do not. I put them because those who make a fetish of the changeable press them; as if those who do not, thereby belittle the need for social change. And it is right that we be clear in this. Since Blake believed that man's imagination is timeless and of the same shape, he may be pressed to mean that it lasts more than a thousand years, a thousand ages, the lifetime of the earth. This seems reasonable. Nevertheless, the reasoning is false. To step from the time scale of history to that of evolution, and thence to that of geology, is not merely to lengthen our stride. It is to cross thresholds from quantity to quality. The thoughts and feelings which we share with the men of China, of Troy, and of Ur; and those which we share with our ape forefathers of a million generations back; these do not differ merely in number, but in kind. The kinds of thought and feeling, the kind of truth, to which Blake held and for which we read him, lie within historical times. They are not therefore impermanent. The point has been made in his own way by an orthodox materialist, Christopher Caudwell.

> Great art – art which performs a wide and deep feat of integration – has something universal, something timeless and enduring from age to age. This timelessness we now see to be the timelessness of the instincts, the unchanging secret face of the genotype, which persists beneath all the rich super-structure of civilisation.

This is Blake's thought, in his own image. Societies have changed much in historical times, but the men within them and those who remade them have held their deepest thoughts and feelings steadfastly. They have held them in virtue of being men, in body and in mind together: 'the unchanging secret face of the genotype', the Human Form Divine. In the tools which men have made, in the forces which these tools unleashed, in the new societies made by these forces, they have sought always to fulfil their unchanging manhood: that imagination which makes them alike Benjamin Franklin's tool-making animal and Blake's 'Poetic Genius'. Adam Smith spoke for a changing society when he invented the economics of supply and demand. The society had long spoken his thought, in using the word Dearth to mean dearness and scarcity together. But across all societies, man speaks for himself in his own image, in his steadfast use of the words Dexterous and Sinister, Adroit and Gauche: in his use of the word Right. Man with a vertical plane of near-symmetry who walks upright and uses his hands for tools is fixed to ways of seeing, of thinking, and of behaving which time cannot change unless it changes him, and until it makes him something else than man. Man who sees and thinks in three dimensions, whose reasoning is grounded on true and false alone, and who feels loneliness, love, and pity as passions, is fixed to a shape of mind which is absolute for his kind. Socially, man with ten fingers will make the commandments and the decimal system. As a man, the man of reason and passion held in one will write *Gulliver's Travels* and *The Song of Los*. Blake saw that man as one, and saw 'the timelessness of the instincts' as a more moving force towards truth.

> The truth & certainty of Virtue & Honesty, *i.e.* Inspiration, needs no one to prove it; it is Evident as the Sun & Moon. He who stands doubting of what he intends, whether it is Virtuous or Vicious, knows not what Virtue means. No man can do a Vicious action & think it to be Virtuous. No man can take darkness for light.
>
> 386

SIX

Poems move men in society, as well as man alone. For their language moves, as well as that which it says. And since the tasks of language are social, societies have looked askance where they have seen it most moving. Watchfully they have asked, How far is the end of poems that of all language, to get things changed? When does literature make propaganda?

Writers who have not shared Blake's fate, to live under a censorship, have commonly turned this question upside down. They have been troubled to find, and they have asked why it is, that propaganda seldom makes literature. I think that this is an easier question. Propaganda has for its aim the changing of society to serve one interest in place of another. Those whose interest is to be served seldom need propaganda to tell them so. Propaganda must make the new society seem comfortable to men who have less to gain. It must be planned nicely and differently for each set of such men. And the proselytizing religions, and the doctrinaire parties, use writers who plan precisely for each set of hearers. Like those who sell drink, tobacco, and patent medicines, they give different reasons to the man in the bar and the gentleman in the parlour. Writing designed to give such striking and short-lived reasons for discontent to each class in turn does not seek, and seldom finds, the simple truths with manifold meanings to which the mind comes back. *Uncle Tom's Cabin* and *Lady Chatterley's Lover* fail in this way, with *The Drapier's Letters* and *Rerum Novarum*. They linger not as literature, which is lasting because it is truthful, but as monuments to social discontent. There is a propaganda which tries to speak to more hearers, by counting out the great truths like lead florins: Lincoln used it at Gettysburg, before Hitler at the Sportpalast. It is as false, because it hides the social interests at odds as lavishly. When Pericles spoke of the Athenian dead, he began soberly at the causes of the war with Sparta. But Lincoln did not recall Federation and Negro Slavery.

Writers of literature have their own vested interest. Whether they wish it or not, they write propaganda for it. And this is why societies have feared them. The fear seems odd to us: literature has few readers, and what it says to them does not seem urgent. What is its propaganda? What had Pitt to fear from such men as Blake? What had Walpole to fear from Swift and Pope?

> *Friend.* Tis all a Libel – *Paxton* (Sir) will say. ⎫
> *Poet.* Not yet, my Friend! to-morrow 'faith it may; ⎬
> And for that very cause I print to day. ⎭
> How shou'd I fret, to mangle ev'ry line,
> In rev'rence to the Sins of *Thirty-nine!*

The questions remain apt, since 1939 does not seem to have moved far from 1739.

The plain answer is, that Walpole wished to silence Swift and Pope because they were Tories in a Whig society; and Pitt wished to silence Blake and his fellows, because they were Radicals in a Tory society. This answer is too plainly true to be new. Nevertheless, it has been better understood by the designers of states than by the writers of literature. For this is as much why Hitler exiled men trained in science from his state, as why Plato exiled poets from his. *Mein Kampf* gives this reason more roundly than *The Republic*.

> The object of propaganda is to compel the whole people to accept a doctrine.

Our organization only admits into its ranks those whose psychological make-up is such that they do not threaten to become an obstacle to the further spread of our idea.

In this meaning, Marxist critics justly claim that all great writers have been revolutionary, because they have spoken against the class then in power. But they have not always spoken for the class then fighting towards power: Swift and Pope did not. What makes great writers one is not dissent looking forward, but dissent itself, in the widest meaning. This is why the designers of Utopias, of whatever kind, have feared their cast of mind more than their writings. If you want to run a state for ever without trouble, says Plato, says Hitler, get rid of those whose make-up is odd, questioning, dissenting. Get rid of truth, get rid of literature, because their common interest is dissent.

If this is just, then it is plain why literature seldom makes propaganda for some one social change. It is plain why great writers have written, as Blake did, in fear of the societies towards which they themselves fought, as well as of those in which they were prisoners. And it is plain why, in thought and manner, they spent their lives in tireless experiment, as Blake did, as Swift and Pope did, and as small writers do not. Literature can make propaganda for a social plan. But it can do so, and be literature, only by feeling within that plan the passion of its own dissent. It can do so only by giving to the hunger of a class for power or for bread the restless urgency of the writer's own hunger for another self. Blake did this at times; and Shelley did not.

SEVEN

The cast of mind which searches, which questions, which dissents, has a great history. Each society has given it its own form: religious, literary, scientific. Much of the strength of Blake derives from the twofold form which dissent took in his time: rational and inspired. But however it has been made, this has been the ferment which has quickened societies. It was homely in the men who gave a history in one pattern to the merchant societies, first of Holland and then of England. The discoveries which used the raw stuffs which Holland lacked, to take England beyond this pattern, were made by men of the same mind. And this was the cast of mind of the great Russian writers in whom the social revolution to come first spoke. There is truth, the truth of dissent, in the unfinished verses which Blake wrote with this thought.

> 'Now Art has lost its mental Charms
> France shall subdue the World in Arms.'
> So spoke an Angel at my birth,
> Then said, 'Descend thou upon Earth.
> Renew the Arts on Britain's Shore,
> And France shall fall down & adore.
> With works of Art their Armies meet,
> And War shall sink beneath thy feet.
> But if thy Nation Arts refuse,
> And if they scorn the immortal Muse,
> France shall the arts of Peace restore,
> And save thee from the Ungrateful shore.'
>   Spirit, who lov'st Britannia's Isle
> Round which the Fiends of Commerce smile –   **557**

For Blake's cast of mind might indeed have made England one with the French Revolution.

The history of dissent is not yet ended; it does not end. Men die, and societies die. They are not more lasting for being without dissent, they are more brittle: for they are purposeless, because they deny themselves a future. And if at times states are made to work, as all states have wished to work, without dissent, they are the poorer. They may be richer for a time than the pitiful starved societies which men have made hitherto; but they are poorer than they might themselves be. Men who are denied the right to dissent are no longer full men, and do not make a society worthy as men: 'they seem to me to be something Else besides Human Life.' The right to ask and to be answered, truth; the right to judge and to choose, dignity; these, and justice, and pity, and love, and reason, are of the shape of man's mind. These drive him to shape as a shadow the societies in which he must try, and will fail, to fulfil himself. Their dissent gives him the hope, their dissent alone gives him the power, to fail by less.

Societies may set themselves other ends: power for one class, freedom for many, happiness, use. None of these models is good, none has even a meaning, unless it takes it from the hope of fulfilment of what makes man man and not beast: the whole range of his mind, from the *reductio ad absurdum* to passion. The greatest of social critics, Karl Marx, believed that the society for which he fought was shaped by the needs of history itself, to put an end to the waste of the well-being of men. This is no less a myth than Blake's Jerusalem, and no less noble. Both are driven by the same loves and indignations. We cannot read the moving work of Marx without feeling the more passionate needs which drove him to write it, and which make us tremble in the reading as he shook in the writing: the pity, the anger, the grief, and the horror of a society in which men who work go poor. The Labour Theory of Value is not a piece of reasoning, because value is not a measure accessible to bargaining. It is the claim of the imagination to the Rights of Man: that he who does has a right to plenty, juster than the power of him who owns to hold him in famine. It is of a piece with that poem in which, precisely, Blake spoke propaganda and dissent in one.

> Shall not the King call for Famine from the heath,
> Nor the Priest for Pestilence from the fen,
> To restrain, to dismay, to thin
> The inhabitants of mountain and plain,
> In the day of full-feeding prosperity
> And the night of delicious songs?
>   Shall not the Councellor throw his curb
> Of Poverty on the laborious,
> To fix the price of labour,
> To invent allegoric riches?
>   And the privy admonishers of men
> Call for fires in the City,
> For heaps of smoking ruins
> In the night of prosperity & wantonness?
>   To turn man from his path,
> To restrain the child from the womb,
> To cut off the bread from the city,
> That the remnant may learn to obey,
>   That the pride of the heart may fail,
> That the lust of the eyes may be quench'd,

> That the delicate ear in its infancy
> May· be dull'd, and the nostrils clos'd up,
> To teach mortal worms the path
> That leads from the gates of the Grave.   247

Within the great work of Marx sounds the greater cry for the dignity of labour. Behind it rages the more pitiless will to truth. He fought for a society which should be good, that men might fulfil these and themselves. And he did not lose the hope, that there that which ranges society against man might wither away.

We shall not see the fulfilment of his hope. Like Blake, I do not think that a society can fulfil it. But we can honour the wish which gave the hope: to make man and not society master. This is the wish which has driven great poets, of whom Blake was one. They wore their pride in this wish like an affront. And their dissent was an affront to their societies. Yet they wore it with assurance, because they knew it rooted, not in the struggle of men to make the most of their neighbours, but in the shape of man's mind. Alike in his prophetic books and in his poems, Blake spoke this wish with ruthless single-mindedness, because he believed that he spoke the truths of this mind. These truths do not make a large show; and the long misuse of rant has worn them shabby. Thomas Love Peacock, who was a shrewd judge of the nature of poetry, found it easy to belittle them in Blake's lifetime:

> only the more tangible points of morality, those which command assent at once, those which have a mirror in every mind.

Such are the root thoughts which have been held in common, for some thousands of years, by minds which have been happy enough to miss the endless mutilations of poverty and indignity. They speak of man in love, in need, in thought, in passion. They speak of man bounded by all these, yet driven to speak by them, and able to speak only in them. They speak for man beset by his shortcomings, yet seeking an ideal which must be shadowed in the actual; which societies wrong, but which must act in society; which words betray, but which must speak or be lost. They speak two words: truth the ideal, and dignity the search for its ful· filment. It is not a large show; but it puts a world to shame.

EIGHT

Blake was a poor man, and he suffered wrongs and indignities. An age conspired to defeat him; it cowed him, but it did not break him. The sympathy with the French Revolution; the sympathy with the poor; the twofold, self-fulfilling truth which innocence must renew in experience: these at last are one, in the great and simple man who died as he had lived, a craftsman at his work. He had written humbly that—

> Resentment for Personal Injuries has had some share in this Public Address, But Love to My Art & Zeal for my Country a much Greater. 594

And truthfully and without bitterness, the public and the private life become one, when he writes of himself, his art, and his time,

> A Last Judgment is Necessary because Fools flourish. Nations Flourish under Wise Rulers & are depress'd under foolish Rulers; it is the same with Individuals as Nations; works of Art can only be produc'd in Perfection where the Man is either in Affluence or is Above the Care of it. Poverty is the Fool's Rod, which at last is turn'd on his own back; this is A Last Judgment – when Men of Real Art Govern & Pretenders Fall. Some People & not a few Artists have asserted that the Painter of this Picture would not have done so well if he had been properly Encourag'd. Let those who think so, reflect on the State of Nations under Poverty & their incapability of Art; tho' Art is Above Either, the Argument is better for Affluence than Poverty; & tho' he would not have been a greater Artist, yet he would have produc'd Greater works of Art in proportion to his means. A Last Judgment is not for the purpose of making Bad Men better, but for the Purpose of hindering them from opressing the Good with Poverty & Pain by means of Such Vile Arguments & Insinuations. 612

This has the ease, the dignity, and the single mind of a great writer: a truth and a generosity which confound an age. This at last is to understand Blake: when we see as one, the vision of indignation in the prophetic mask, and Pity the Human Face of the *Songs of Innocence*. Nearly thirty years after Blake's death the painter Samuel Palmer recalled him, 'his aim single, his path straightforwards, and his wants few; so he was free, noble, and happy.' He put the memory of Blake into one phrase—

> He was a man without a mask.

I can add nothing to this epitaph.

NOTES

✦❧✦

THE TURBULENT AGE, 4: pages 8–9. The best balanced account of the Town and its patronage in Augustan times is in Leslie Stephen's *English Literature and Society in the Eighteenth Century.*

5: page 11. John Locke's *Essay Concerning Human Understanding* was almost a humanist bible in the dissenting academies; it had great influence on Joseph Priestley and, in turn, on his students. By contrast, it was anathema in the universities; Oxford students had been forbidden to read it in 1703. See Irene Parker, *Dissenting Academies in England.*

I have taken the story of Gillray's cartoon and Blake's use of it from David Erdman's *Blake: Prophet Against Empire.* This is the most important book that has been written about Blake in recent years.

6: pages 11–14. My sketch of Blake's place in the Gnostic tradition of dissent is based on *The Everlasting Gospel* by A. L. Morton. There is a detailed exposition of the beliefs and writings of the Brethren of the Free Spirit (the Ranters), in their chiliastic context, in *The Pursuit of the Millennium* by Norman Cohn.

The lasting influence of the sects on education was foreseen by the antiquary Anthony Wood in 1659: 'But in these late times when the dregs of people grew wiser than their teachers and . . . therefore above all religion ordinarily profest, nothing could satisfie their insatiable desires but aiming at an utter subversion of them, church and schools. . . . And as it was a common matter to declaime against universities in publicke, soe was it also in the private meetings and conventicles of Anabaptists, Quakers and such like unstable people.'

6: page 13. Blake's usage is very up to date. The word 'gas' (which had been coined earlier by the Flemish chemist van Helmont from the Greek χάος) was first used in English in its modern sense in 1779, five years before Blake began *An Island in the Moon.* Priestley, who had discovered oxygen in 1774, had called it not 'inflammable gas' but 'dephlogisticated air'. Blake knew about this too; elsewhere in *An Island in the Moon* he makes Priestley cry in panic, at the escape of an unhealthy gas, 'Our lungs are destroy'd with the Flogiston'. (Compare *Dissent*, 4: page 142.)

THE PROPHETIC MASK, 1: page 23. This print, from *The Oxford Magazine*, is shown in W. P. Treloar's *Wilkes and the City*.

2: pages 24–7. The reader should be warned that my judgement of Blake's designs is not shared by many more knowledgeable critics. Of their judgements, the most enlightening has seemed to me to be that of Ewan Phillips, in his thesis *English Expressionist Artists in the Nineteenth Century*. I am sorry to learn that this has not been printed.

2: page 25. The quotation is from Hogarth's own notes of his life.

2: page 26. The plate in Erasmus Darwin's *The Botanic Garden* which I had in mind is the well-known *Fertilization of Egypt*. But I learn that one edition of the book, the rare third edition, in fact has a second plate *Typhoon* engraved by Blake after Fuseli. I am indebted to Ruthven Todd for telling me this and much else. Blake also engraved four plates which show the Portland vase for Darwin's book in 1791.

3: page 27. Henry Crabb Robinson in 1825 wrote of his conversations with Blake, 'When he said "*my visions*" it was in the ordinary unemphatic tone in which we speak of trivial matters that every one understands and cares nothing about. In the same tone he said repeatedly: "The Spirit told me." '

6: page 34. I have taken the text of Thomas Butts's letter, here and on page 109, from Mona Wilson's *Life of William Blake*.

6: page 36. The prose quotation is from A. E. Housman's *The Name and Nature of Poetry*.

7: page 38. The quotation from Swinburne here, as well as the words quoted on page 77, are from *William Blake, A Critical Essay*.

THE SEDITIOUS WRITINGS: *Trade*. The matter of this chapter and of the chapters headed *Machines* and *Dissent* has needs been taken from many sources, ranging from standard histories to research notes. I list, and quote, only the more general; I hope that the reader who is drawn to these will follow the fuller references which they give.

3: page 47. The lines by Edward Young are quoted in Samuel Johnson's life of him. The first quotation from Swift is from a letter to Pope; the second from *The Conduct of the Allies*.

3: pages 48–9. The verses by Pope here and on pages 64 and 187 are taken from his Satires.

4: pages 49–52. As everywhere in these chapters, I am indebted here to W. E. H. Lecky's great *History of England in the Eighteenth Century*. But the largest debt of this section is to M. Dorothy George's vivid *London Life in the Eighteenth Century*. Francis Place's recollection, quoted on page 52, is taken from the latter, as well as the report of the Foundling Hospital which I quote on page 149. There is a readable account of many of these matters in *Johnson's England*, edited by A. S. Turberville, from which I have taken John Freeth's couplet on page 151.

The first quotation on page 49 is from Locke's second treatise *Of Civil Government*; the second from Adam Smith's *The Wealth of Nations*.

5: page 53. I quote the text of George III's letters here from Edward Lascelles's *Life of Charles James Fox*. I have taken other texts from this book on pages 72, 73, and 84. Queen Victoria's letter was written to Sir Henry Ponsonby.

6: page 56. The prose quotations are from the *Works* of Edmund Burke, from which I also quote on pages 99–100, 103, and 152.

Alexander Gilchrist notes that Blake engraved four pictures for the book of John Scott's poems in which *The Drum* was printed. (At one time these were thought to be the work of another engraver of the same name, who was a Freemason. Compare 5: page 54.)

6: page 58. When Blake in later life, after several changes, engraved the pencil drawing of *The Accusers*, or *Our End Is Come* (Plate 10), he called one of its three figures *The Executioner*, and gave him a sword, a Roman face, and a laurel crown.

7: pages 59–61. The facts are given in J. P. De Castro's *The Gordon Riots*, from which I have quoted Benjamin Franklin's letter on page 60 (17 June 1780). There are also some striking pages on the riots in Leonard Woolf's *After the Deluge*. I do not, however, share the view of either writer on the causes of the riots. See also *The Crowd in History, 1730–1848* by George Rudé, and his article on the riots.

The quotation on page 59 is from a marginal note by Franklin; that on page 61, from the Declaration of Independence.

The Seditious Writings, 1: page 62. David Erdman in *Blake: Prophet Against Empire* shows that *Glad Day* is a misnomer: the picture is more aptly called *Albion Rose*; and he gives reasons to think that it symbolizes such a rising as the Gordon riots.

2: page 68. I have discussed the fascination of the crime story, in the eighteenth century and since, in an essay in my book *The Face of Violence*. (Compare also *Trade*, 4: page 52.)

3: page 70. The quotation is from Élie Halévy's *History of the English People in 1815*. I am indebted to this scrupulous book throughout the chapters which follow. In particular, I have quoted texts from it on pages 74, 101, 106, 146, and 174.

4: pages 72–4. The last quotation on page 73 is from Charles Whibley's *William Pitt*; the first on page 74, from notes which Mary Wollstonecraft sent from France to Joseph Johnson (Paris, 15 February 1793).

Since writing these pages, I have found this legislation admirably summarized in G. D. H. Cole's essay *A Study in Legal Repression*, in his collection *Persons and Periods*.

5: page 77. Lord Ellenborough's letter is printed in *Private Papers of William Wilberforce*, edited by A. M. Wilberforce. Among these papers is Wilberforce's Character of Pitt, from which I quote in passing on page 73, and the letter from George Rose which I quote on page 104.

THE SATANIC WHEELS: *Machines*, 1: page 89. This quotation from Pitt is given by J. L. Hammond and Barbara Hammond in *The Town Labourer 1760–1832*. I am indebted to this and the other vigorous books of these writers, *The Village Labourer 1760–1832*, *The Skilled Labourer 1760–1832*, in many places: in particular, for the text of quotations on pages 98, 104, 144–5, 146, and 149.

1: page 90. The letter from Matthew Boulton quoted, here, and other letters quoted on page 95, are printed by H. W. Dickinson and Rhys Jenkins in *James Watt and the Steam Engine*.

2: pages 90–2. Here and elsewhere, I owe much to Paul Mantoux's masterly account of *The Industrial Revolution in the Eighteenth Century*, from which I quote texts on pages 93, 99, and 141.

5: pages 96–7. This story and the comment are from George Unwin's *Samuel Oldknow and the Arkwrights*, which is also the source of the quotation on page 102. My references to Defoe are, of course, to his *Tour through England and Wales*.

5: page 98. The poets had no notion that the rich were enclosing the common land for profit; they thought it was for pleasure. So Goldsmith wrote:

> But times are altered; trade's unfeeling train
> Usurp the land and dispossess the swain;
> Along the lawn, where scattered hamlets rose,

Unwieldy wealth, and cumbrous pomp repose;
And every want to luxury allied,
And every pang that folly pays to pride.

5: page 99. So Boswell quotes Johnson, in his *Life of Samuel Johnson*.

6: pages 101–2. (See also 3: pages 93–4.) Pictures and details of these and other tokens are given by F. D. Klingender, *Eighteenth Century Pence and Ha'pence*, in *The Architectural Review* for February 1943.

6: page 103. The quotations are from Byron's *Vision of Judgment*.

7: page 105. The quotation from Swift is from *The Drapier's Fourth Letter*.

The Satanic Wheels, 1 and 2: pages 107–13. The account of Blake's trial in the *Sussex Advertiser*, from which I quote on page 107, and John Scholfield's deposition, from which I quote on page 112, have been given in a number of places: among others, in Mona Wilson's *Life of William Blake*. The indictment, from which I quote on page 111, is given by Herbert Jenkins in his book of studies, *William Blake*. It is often said that Blake was tried for high treason, and might have been hanged. The indictment and the jury's finding show that this is not so.

3: page 115. The quotation from Humphry Davy is from his *Discourse Introductory to a Course of Lectures on Chemistry*.

4 and 5: pages 116–24. I now find that the industrial imagery in Blake was remarked by Harold Bruce in 1925 in *Blake in This World* —a pioneer book which has been neglected.

5 and 6: pages 123–6. Adam Smith in *The Wealth of Nations* had also pointed to the consequences of the division of labour as Blake did, but without Blake's passion: 'The man whose whole life is spent in performing a few simple operations, of which the effects too are, perhaps, always the same, or very nearly the same, has no occasion to exert his understanding, or to exercise his invention in finding out expedients for removing difficulties which never occur. He naturally loses, therefore, the habit of such exertion, and generally becomes as stupid and ignorant as it is possible for a human creature to become. The torpor of his mind renders him, not only incapable of relishing or bearing a part in any rational conversation, but of conceiving any generous, noble, or tender sentiment.'

6: page 126. Here and elsewhere, on pages 57, 62, 64, 150–4, and 164–5, I have tried to choose poems to which the reader can turn readily in *The Oxford Book of Eighteenth Century Verse*, edited by David Nichol Smith.

6: pages 127–8. T. S. Ashton in *The Industrial Revolution 1760–1830* writes: 'More than 200 years earlier, the State had made provision for the regulation of labour, and, though the statutes were now rarely enforced, it was held that to seek to increase wages, other than by appeal to the Justices, was illegal or even a crime. So long as a union remained passive it was left undisturbed, but the outbreak of a dispute was often the occasion for the employers to petition for an Act to put down combination in the trade concerned. Before the end of the century the number of such pieces of legislation (not all of which, however, were enforced) exceeded forty; and in 1799 the master millwrights of London, at odds with their men, were seeking yet another Act of this kind. Britain was at war: the ruling classes feared that unions might serve as a cloak for corresponding societies or other, more revolutionary, bodies. When, therefore, Wilberforce proposed that the millwrights' Bill should be extended to cover workers in all occupations, opposition was small. The Act of 1799 laid down that any person who joined with another to obtain an increase of wages or a reduction of hours might be brought before a magistrate and, on conviction, sentenced to three months in prison.' Compare *Machines*, 1: page 89.

6: page 128. The quotation is from a letter written by R. L. Edgeworth to Anne Romily, on 6 February 1816.

INNOCENCE AND EXPERIENCE: *Dissent*, 1: pages 135–7. The matter of these pages and kindred matters are treated by Anthony Blunt in two scholarly articles on Blake in the *Warburg Journal*, II (1938–9), pages 53–63 and 65–8. I am indebted to these articles, although I do not wholly share their view.

1: page 136. Dorothy Plowman, in introducing a facsimile of *The Book of Urizen* in 1929, and Frederick E. Pierce, in the *Philological Quarterly* in 1931, have suggested that Blake made up the name Urizen from the Ionic form οὐρίζειν of the Greek verb ὁρίζειν, to bound or limit. This is far-fetched; Blake was still trying to learn Greek almost ten years later, at Felpham in 1803; so that, if he met the Greek root at all, it was more likely (as David Erdman implies) in the English word 'horizon'. But all these speculations miss the crux of Blake's symbol, which is that *Your reason* in the sense of Priestley's challenge is the boundary that limits and confines human energy. (See THE

TURBULENT AGE, 6: pages 13–14.) I repeat the important passage which I have quoted from *The Marriage of Heaven and Hell*: 'Reason is the bound or outward circumference of Energy. Energy is Eternal Delight.'

2: pages 138–9. I had at first taken it for granted that Blake was thinking of the space outside a small sphere and inside a larger. On putting these two boundaries over each other, he would get a solid analogue of the surface of a ring. But M. H. A. Newman, who kindly read what I had written, writes: 'Isn't Blake really thinking of the solid analogue of the surface of a sphere? Reasoning (quite correctly) by analogy, he thinks of a small circle starting at the North Pole, and broadening out till it reaches the Mundane Shell, the equator, where it has its maximum possible extent, and where the surface is still "within and without". Going on still further we eventually come to the "vortex"—the South Pole: and "everything has its own vortex" —its antipodes. All this goes perfectly in one dimension higher, on the solid analogue of the surface of a sphere.' I now incline to this reading of Blake. Blake had read about vortices, of course, in translations of Descartes.

3: pages 139–41. Other views, no less well founded than mine, may be found, on the one hand in B. Hessen's article 'The Social and Economic Roots of Newton's Principia', printed in *Science at the Cross Roads*; and on the other, in G. N. Clark's *Science and Social Welfare in the Age of Newton*.

4: pages 141–3. The topic of this section is treated at length in my book (with Bruce Mazlish) *The Western Intellectual Tradition*. Details of the work of many of these men are given briefly in A. Wolf's *History of Science, Technology and Philosophy in the Eighteenth Century*. There is now a full study of *The Lunar Society of Birmingham* by Robert Schofield, and a lucid essay by Eric Robinson.

5: pages 143–5. There is an account of Priestley's writings in Basil Willey's *The Eighteenth Century Background*. This book treats a number of other writings which I have quoted, among them those of Godwin and Wordsworth's *Letter to the Bishop of Llandaff*. I have taken the text of quotations on pages 78, 84, and 130 from it. Neither this nor other books, however, capture the range of influence of Priestley and his dissenting friends: their originality dominated science as well as education towards the end of the eighteenth century. For example, Priestley showed (from an observation of Benjamin Franklin's) that electric charges obey the law of inverse squares, and he published the first account of colour-blindness. Richard Price edited a paper by another Unitarian minister, Thomas Bayes, after his death, which for two hundred years has remained the most powerful and controversial contribution to the modern theory of probability.

5: page 144. My reference is, of course, to R. H. Tawney's *Religion and the Rise of Capitalism*, and the work of Max Weber.

6: page 145. The quotation is from John Telford's *Life of John Wesley*.

7: pages 147–50. I owe my knowledge of the child cult, and of much else in Blake, to many talks with John Danby, to whom I should like to record my great debt. The evangelical background of the *Songs of Innocence* has also been stressed by E. M. W. Tillyard, and by John Sampson in his edition of *The Poetical Works of William Blake*.

Innocence and Experience, 2: page 155. Kathleen Raine has pointed out to me that Blake had been reading Jacob Boehme's *Aurora*: 'Most certainly there is but one God; but when the veil is put away from thy eyes, so that thou seest and knowest him, then thou wilt also see and know *all* thy Brethren, whether they be Christians, Jews, Turks or Heathens. Or dost thou think that God is the God of you Christians only?'

7: page 169. The prose quotations are from Genesis 22, 17 and from Numbers 24, 5 and 6.

THE MAN WITHOUT A MASK, 2: pages 177–8. A. L. Morton in *The Everlasting Gospel* has pointed out that the Ranters, and other Anabaptist sects, were accused of going naked, and surely did so at times. Blake's views on nakedness and on sex were of a piece with theirs, and were plainly put in his poems and in his speech. On 13 June 1826 (a year before he died) Blake told Henry Crabb Robinson that women should be held in common; Robinson was so shocked that he wrote the entry in his diary in German: 'He says that from the Bible he has learned that *Eine Gemeinschaft der Frauen Statt finden sollte.*'

The critic who based his understanding of Blake on the belief that Blake was oversexed was Herbert Jenkins.

5: page 185. The quotation is from Christopher Caudwell's *Illusion and Reality*.

7: page 191. The quotation is from Peacock's *Four Ages of Poetry*.

INDEX

❦